Foundational Beliefs:
A Christian Study
Guide

by

Rev. R. Nathaniel Mitchell

authorHOUSE®

AuthorHouse™
1663 Liberty Drive
Bloomington, IN 47403
www.authorhouse.com
Phone: 1 (800) 839-8640

Published by AuthorHouse   05/21/2016

ISBN: 978-1-4343-6671-9 (sc)
ISBN: 978-1-5049-7247-5 (e)

Print information available on the last page.

Any people depicted in stock imagery provided by Thinkstock are models, and such images are being used for illustrative purposes only. Certain stock imagery © Thinkstock.

This book is printed on acid-free paper.

Scripture quotations marked KJV are from the Holy Bible, King James Version (Authorized Version). First published in 1611. Quoted from the KJV Classic Reference Bible, Copyright © 1983 by The Zondervan Corporation.

Dedication

This project is dedicated to the Memory and Ministry of
Rev. Dr. & Mrs. Melvin J. (Katherin T.) Mitchell
Of Columbus, Ohio

To the Memories of

Mr. & Mrs. Edward L. (Janie L.) Thomas,
Of Youngstown, Ohio

And the

Mt Sinai Baptist Church
6850 Plainfield Road
Silverton (Cincinnati), Ohio 45236

Table of Contents

Appreciation

Many thanks to those people who provided encouragement; who assisted using their editorial skills, and to the Mt. Sinai Baptist Church, where God allowed me to develop and hone my pastoral skills, in order to bring souls to Christ. Most of all, we thank Almighty God for his manifold blessings and unending grace.

The Pledge
to the
Bible

I Pledge allegiance to the Bible,
God's Holy Word. I will make it a
lamp unto my feet, and a light
unto my pathway. I will hide its
words in my heart; that I
might not sin against
God.

How to Use This Workbook

I. To effectively use this study workbook, you will need several tools:
1. an active prayer life
2. a study Bible
3. a Bible concordance
4. Bible dictionary
5. a Webster's Dictionary
6. note paper
7. writing utensils

With the above tools, you will have adequate reference materials on hand.

II. PRAY to the Lord Jesus, asking for humility, courage, guidance, obedience and greater understanding of the Word of God.

III. In each chapter you will be asked questions and provided with texts related to the answers. Read each question or statement thoroughly. Then using the text, research the information in the Bible. Write the answer or scripture (where applicable) in the space provided. Often, more than one scripture is given for clarity. Be certain to read each scripture to get a clearer understanding.

Included is an area for note-taking while you study each chapter. Be sure to write down questions to investigate or ask your local pastor/teacher during class study time.

IV. Check Your Answers

When you have successfully completed a chapter (only after filling in every blank), check your answers against the answer key at the back of this workbook. Be sure to always correct all wrong answers, and go back to reference materials to discover why the key is correct. If there are still unresolved questions, write them down and seek answers from your local pastor/teacher. God Bless you!

* NOTE: DO NOT BE DISCOURAGED IF YOU DO NOT KNOW ANSWERS! Remember, this is a study guide, so it does take some investigation. The whole idea is to learn more about God and Christianity.

CHAPTER ONE:

What Christians Believe About...

God, the CREATOR

Find and write the answers for each question!

1. God is self-existent. (Gen. 1:1; Ex. 3:13-14)

_____

_____

_____

_____

_____

_____

_____

2. God is Omnipotent (all powerful). (Gen. 18:14; Rev. 19:6)

_____

_____

_____

_____

_____

3. God is Omnipresent (ever-present). (Ps. 139:7-12)

_____

_____

_____

_____

_____

_____

4. God is Omniscient (all-knowing). (Ps. 139:2-6; Isa. 40:13-14)

_____

_____

_____

_____

_____

_____

5. God is Immutable (unchangeable). (Heb. 1:10-12; 13:8)

_____

_____

_____

_____

_____

6. God is Infinite (all). (1 Ki. 8:22-27; Jer. 23:24)

_____

_____

_____

_____

_____

_____

7. God is Eternal. (Deut. 33:27; Ps. 90:2)

_____

_____

_____

_____

_____

8. God is Holy. (Lev. 19:2; 1 Pe. 1:15)

_____

_____

_____

_____

_____

_____

9. God is a Trinity (Three-In-One). (Mt. 28:19; 2 Cor. 13:14)

_____

_____

_____

_____

_____

10. God is a Spirit. (Jn. 4:24)

_____

_____

_____

11. God is the Creator of the universe. (Gen. 1:1)

_____

_____

_____

_____

12. God is the Father of our Lord and Saviour, Jesus Christ. (Jn. 3:16)

_____

_____

_____

_____

13. Is belief in God enough? (circle one) YES OR NO If not, what more is there? Explain!

_____

_____

_____

_____

_____

14. Many people are confused about the "name" of God. God has many names which describe some of His magnificent multitude of functions manifested upon mankind. Below are ten (10) Hebrew names and functions of God. (Be sure to read each accompanying scripture)

Name	Meaning	Refers to	Scripture
1. Elohim	God	God's power and might	Gen. 1:1; Ps. 19:1
2. Jehovah (also Yahweh)	Lord	God's divine salvation	Gen. 2:4
3. Adonai	Lord	Lordship of God	Mal. 1:6
4. Jehovah-Rohi	The Lord is my shepherd		Ps. 23:1
5. Jehovah-Rapha	The Lord our healer		Ex. 16:26
6. Jehovah-Tsidkenu	The Lord our righteous		Jer. 23:6
7. Jehovah-Jireh	The Lord will provide		Gen. 22:13-14
8. Jehovah-Nissi	The Lord our banner		Ex. 17:15
9. Jehovah-Shalom	The Lord is peace		Judges 6:24
10. El-Shaddai	God Almighty		Gen. 17:1; Ps. 91:1

Special Reference Notes

CHAPTER TWO:
What Christians Believe About ...
SALVATION

1. What is salvation?

    _____

    _____

    _____

2. Who was salvation originally intended to benefit? (Jn. 1:11)

    _____

    _____

3. Why is salvation necessary?

    _____

    _____

4. From where does salvation come? OR By what method has salvation come
    into the world? (Jn. 3:16)

    _____

    _____

    _____

    _____

5. Did God plan salvation? (Acts 4:10-12)

    _____

    _____

    _____

    _____

    _____

6. How is salvation manifested in this world? (Jn. 3:17-18)

_____

_____

_____

_____

7. Will everyone on earth receive salvation? YES or NO (circle one)

_____

_____

_____

8. Is there a specific age when one should be saved? YES or NO (circle one)

_____

_____

_____

9. How is someone saved... or ...by what authority is one saved? (Acts 4:12)

_____

_____

_____

10. Once saved, can anyone lose that salvation? YES or NO (circle one) If yes, Explain how !

_____

_____

_____

11. What is the ultimate benefit in becoming saved?

_____

_____

_____

12. How does John 3:16 come into the picture of salvation?

_____

_____

_____

_____

13. What part does Calvary (Golgotha) play in salvation? (Lk. 23:33)

_____

_____

_____

_____

14. Can we be saved without faith in Jesus Christ?   YES   or   NO   (circle one) EXPLAIN!

_____

_____

_____

15. What is the most prominent Christian symbol of salvation?

_____

_____

_____

16. Can salvation come by merit or works? YES or NO (circle one) EXPLAIN! (also see #22)

_____

_____

_____

_____

17. What must occur inwardly for salvation to take place? (Jn. 3:3)

_____

_____

_____

_____

18. What it meant by being "born again" (Jn. 3)?

_____

_____

_____

_____

_____

19. Is a belief in Jesus Christ essential to salvation, or is a belief in God enough? (Acts 4:1-12)

_____

_____

_____

_____

_____

_____

_____

20. What is the process for salvation? (Rom. 10:9-10)

_____

_____

_____

_____

_____

_____

21. Do "tarrying", speaking in tongues, or "moaners" benches have anything to do with actually being saved? If so, what? EXPLAIN!

_____

_____

_____

_____

_____

22. Can man save himself or anyone else? (Mk. 16:16)

_____

_____

_____

_____

_____

_____

23. Can man be saved by his good works? (Eph. 2:8-9)

_____

_____

_____

_____

_____

_____

24. Can man be saved by baptism alone? (Heb.9:22)

_____

_____

_____

_____

_____

_____

25. Can man be saved by just living? (Gal.2:16, 21; Acts 13:39)

_____

_____

_____

_____

_____

_____

26. Can everybody be saved? (Acts 10:43)

_____

_____

_____

27. Does God want everyone to be saved? (circle one) YES or NO EXPLAIN!
   (2 Pe. 3:9)

_____

_____

_____

_____

28. Did God provided the method of salvation? (1 Jn. 4:10; Rom. 5:8)

_____

_____

_____

_____

_____

_____

_____

29. Can dogs, cats or other lower life animals be saved? (Circle One) **Yes** or **NO**. Why?

_____

_____

_____

_____

_____

_____

_____

_____

_____

_____

_____

_____

_____

_____

Salvation

"Neither is there salvation in any other: for there is none other name under heaven given among men, whereby we must be saved." Acts 4:12

The basic needs of mankind are quite simple; and few in number. Mankind needs food for sustenance, shelter and clothing for safety and security. These three tangibles are quite basic to human existence. There are boundaries and limitations to the realm of these baser necessities. They only satisfy mortal, carnal needs and they do not extend past mortality.

The single most intangible element needed by mankind is salvation for his soul, and from eternal destruction. Certainly we need love, care, tenderness, etc.; but if those never emerge, still salvation is paramount. In the Greek "soteria" is translated "saving", deliverance from and preservation from destruction, and judgment of Noah's flood. "By faith, Noah being warned of God of things not seen as yet, moved with fear, prepared an ark to the saving of his house; by the which he condemned the world, and became heir of the righteousness which is by faith" (Hebrew 11:7).

Mankind needs salvation; that is, man needs to be saved from many worldly entanglements, temptations and negative situations. Mankind needs to be saved from his enemies, that are all around us. They often disguise themselves to look and act like our friends, and others who are earnestly concerned about us. Luke 1:71, concerning the Messiah said, "That we should be saved from our enemies, and from the hand of all that hate us;". Matthew 10:22, "...ye shall be hated of all men for my name's sake: but he that endureth to the end shall be saved". John 15:18, "If the world hates you, ye know that it hated me before it hated you."

We need to be saved from our overt and covert transgressions. Our primary goal in life should be to please God with our new standard of living. God desires that we "resist evil", and be like Jesus Christ in our character. Apostle Paul said in Romans 10:1, "Brethren, my heart's desire and prayer to God for Israel is, that they might be saved". He went on to say in verses 9 and 10, "...if thou shalt confess with thy mouth the Lord Jesus, and shalt believe in thine heart that God hath raised him from the dead, thou shalt be saved." Jesus himself instructed, "Repent, believe and be baptized, and ye shall be saved". We must free ourselves from the conviction of sin, and that can only be accomplished through belief and faith in Jesus Christ.

We need salvation from physical infirmity. In Acts 3:1-12, 16, "…Peter and John went up together into the temple at the hour of prayer…And a certain man lame from his mother's womb was…laid daily to the gate of the temple…called Beautiful to ask alms… he gave heed unto them, expecting to receive something of them. Then Peter said, Silver and gold have I none,…In the name of Jesus Christ of Nazareth rise up and walk. And he took him by the right hand, and lifted him up: and immediately his feet and ankle bones received strength." There is a need for obedience and confidence, if we are to be free from illnesses and sin. Healing is in the hands of the Lord.

We need salvation from the conviction of sin. Luke 19:9-10, "And Jesus said unto him (Zacchaeus), This day is salvation come to this house, forasmuch as he also is a son of Abraham. For the Son of man is come to seek and to save that which was lost". Jesus came to save the Jews first, then everyone; but that particular salvation must come by faith in his precious name. You must "…believe that he is, and that he is a rewarder of those who diligently seek him." Jesus is our Saviour. Second Thessalonians 2:13, "…we are bound to give thanks always to God for you…because God hath from the beginning chosen you to salvation through sanctification of the Spirit and belief of the truth…"

Salvation is that final and complete deliverance from all the curse, including death. It cannot be limited by, or to, the initial stage of redemption; for it is more than the forgiveness of sin. "Salvation in the Bible is translated to mean deliverance, save, health, help, welfare, safety, victory, Saviour, defend, avenge, rescue and preserve" (Finis Dake).

"Neither is there salvation in any other: for there is none other name under heaven given among men, whereby we must be saved." (Acts 4:12). By this scripture you will discover Peter and John, and their unique encounter with a lame man. The man was miraculously healed, and that caused a host of problems for the two apostles in the community and in the temple. The local priests and Sadducees were beside themselves because the apostles "taught the people and preached through Jesus the resurrection of the dead. And they laid hands on them, and put them in hold unto the next day;" (Verses 1-3). Peter and John were physically confined for twenty-four hours, while they contemplated the dilemma. On the next day, they took council against them, and asked, "By what power or by what name, have ye done this? (vs.. 7-8) Then Peter, filled with the Holy Ghost, said unto them; Rulers and elders of the people! If we are being called to account today for an act of kindness shown to a cripple and are asked how he was healed, then know this, you and all the people of Israel: It is by the name of Jesus Christ of Nazareth, whom you crucified, but whom God raised from the dead, that this man stands before you healed.. He is the stone you builders rejected, which has become the capstone. Salvation is found in no one else, for there is none other name under heaven given to men by which we must be saved" (The Daily Bible).

Jesus founded and constructed salvation for the deliverance of mankind. He is "the author and finisher of the faith". The angel declared, "his name shall be called Jesus, for he shall save his people from their sins" (Mt. 1:21). God sent His only Son, and "while we were yet sinners, Christ died for us". His death at the lusty hands of Jewry, established our salvation. Jesus not only died, but he was also raised to life again on the third day morning. His resurrection was the confirmation of our salvation. Then, he ascended back to heaven, and now he sits at the Father's right hand, making intercession for mankind.

Special Reference Notes

CHAPTER THREE:
What Christians Believe About…
SIN

1. What is SIN? (I Jn. 3:4; 5:17)

_____

_____

_____

2. In the light of #1, What is a SINNER?

_____

_____

_____

_____

3. Who is a SINNER? ((Rom. 3:23)

_____

_____

_____

4. When and where was sin introduced into the human family? (Gen. 3:1-9)

_____

_____

_____

4. Who introduced sin into the human family? (Gen. 3:1-6)

(A)_____

(B)_____

(C)_____

5. How was sin introduced into this world? Explain!

_____

_____

6. What are some consequences of sin? (Rom. 5:12; Gen. 3:14-19)
(A)_____ (B)_____ (C)_____ (D)_____ (E)_____

7. What is the fruit of sin? (Rom. 7:5; Gal. 6:7-8)

_____

_____

_____

_____

_____

_____

8. Is the Christian always at war with sin? (Rom. 7:15-24; Gal. 5:17)

_____

_____

_____

_____

_____

_____

_____

9. What is the final punishment for sinning? (Lu. 13:27; Mt. 7:23; 25:41)

_____

_____

_____

_____

10. What causes mankind to sin? (Mt. 13:24-25, 38-39; Jas. 1:14; 4:1-2)

_____

_____

_____

_____

_____

_____

11. How can someone sin by doing nothing? (Jas. 4:17)

_____

_____

_____

_____

_____

_____

12. How are we to overcome sin?. Using the following scriptures, answer this question. (Jas. 4:7; Heb. 2:18, 4:15, 12:3-4; Eph. 6:11-17; Rom. 12:21)

_____

_____

_____

_____

_____

_____

_____

13. Who commits sin? (Rom. 3:23)

_____

_____

14. Can Christians successfully resist temptation? How? (I Cor. 10:13)

_____

_____

_____

15. Can one remain a Christian even though he/she does not always successfully resist temptation? (Acts 8:18-24; Mt. 26:69-75)

_____

_____

_____

_____

_____

_____

_____

16. What does Romans 6:23 confirm about the pay-plan of sin?

_____

_____

_____

17. Does everybody sin? (Rom. 3:10-12)

_____

_____

_____

_____

18. Does man sin by nature? (Ps. 51:5; Eph. 2:3)

_____

_____

_____

_____

19. Does man sin by choice? (Jn. 3:19; Isa. 53:6)

_____

_____

_____

_____

20. Name the two generic types of sin. Man sins by _____
    and by _____.

21. Can any sin be forgiven? YES or NO (circle one)

22. To be forgiven, what must we do?

_____

_____

_____

22. Who is the author and promoter of sin in the earth?

_____

_____

_____

Special Reference Notes

CHAPTER FOUR:
What Christians Believe About...
REPENTANCE *and* FORGIVENESS

1. What is REPENTANCE?

_____

_____

_____

2. Is repentance essential to become a Christian? (Lu. 13:3; Acts 3:1-9; 2 Cor. 7:8-11)

_____

_____

_____

_____

_____

_____

3. Who should repent?

_____

_____

_____

4. What should lead us to repent? (Acts 17:30-31; Lu. 10:13-14; 5:32; Rom. 2:4; 2 Cor. 7:8-11)

_____

_____

_____

_____

_____

5. In the parable of the "prodigal son" (Luke 15), (A) Did he show repentance? If so, (B) When did he repent? (C) How was his affected? (D) Did the elder brother repent? (E) Did the latter have anything of which to repent?

(A)_____

_____

_____

(B)_____

_____

_____

(C)_____

_____

_____

(D)_____

_____

_____

(E)_____

_____

_____

6. What happens when we repent?
Acts 26:20:

_____

_____

Acts 2:38:

_____

_____

Acts 3:19:

_____

_____

Lk. 15:17:

_____

_____

_____

7. Is repentance something we do only once, or is it a continual act to be repeated as often a necessary? (Acts 8:22; Rev. 2:5)

_____

_____

_____

_____

_____

8. What is the act which follows repentance? (Acts 2:38)

_____

_____

_____

_____

_____

9. What is CONVERSION?

_____

_____

_____

_____

_____

10. After repentance and conversion, the believer must become regenerated. Explain the manifestation of a regenerated life. (2 Cor. 5:16-21)

_____

_____

_____

_____

_____

_____

_____

_____

_____

11. What is meant by the axiom..."To err is human, to forgive divine"?

_____
_____
_____
_____
_____
_____
_____

12. Jesus taught forgiveness of our fellowman in the "model prayer" of Mt. 6:12 and Lk. 11:4. Do we have the responsibility to forgive others? What does He say about forgiveness in Mt. 6:14-15, with regard to mankind and the Father?

_____
_____
_____
_____
_____
_____

13. Why did Jesus come to earth? (Jn. 3:16)

_____
_____
_____
_____
_____
_____

14. Conditions of repentance are simple. (Acts 20:21)

_____
_____
_____
_____
_____
_____

15. Turn away from sin and sinning. (Lk. 13:3)

_____

_____

_____

_____

_____

_____

16. Turn toward Jesus. (Jn. 1:12)

_____

_____

_____

_____

_____

_____

17. Completely trust in the Lord. (2 Tim. 1:12; Jn. 6:47)

_____

_____

_____

_____

_____

18. Confess Jesus as your Saviour and Lord. (Rom. 10:9; Mt. 10:32)

_____

_____

_____

_____

_____

_____

19. What should lead us to repent? (Acts 17:30-31; Lk. 10:13-14 5:32; Rom. 2:4; 2 Cor. 7:8-11)

_____

_____

_____

_____

_____

_____

20. How many times must we forgive others? (Mt. 18:21-22)

_____

_____

_____

_____

_____

_____

_____

_____

_____

_____

_____

_____

_____

Special Reference Notes

A Life-Saving Message

"From that time Jesus began to preach, and to say, Repent: for the kingdom of heaven is at hand." (Matthew 4:17)

The main thrust and reason for the gospel message is to save the souls of mankind. Evidently mankind's souls bear great importance to God; because the soul has caused God to sacrifice "his only begotten Son", for the salvation of it. Everybody, at some time or other, has been sorry for doing transgressions. Everybody, at some time or other, has been sorry for doing transgressions. When we came to understand our wrongdoing, and asked forgiveness; we were experiencing the act of repentance.

From Genesis 6:6 through Revelation 16:11, the word *repent* is used 110 times. *REPENTANCE* is important not only to God, but to mankind as well. Momma taught you to apologize, whenever you did anything against anyone. Well, when you transgress the law of God, you should ask Him to forgive you of your sin.

"From that time Jesus began to preach..." Prior to this time, Jesus had not begun his earthly ministry. The last time we heard anything of him, he was 12 years old, in the Jerusalem temple teaching the doctor and lawyers. That is when he stated "...I must be about my Father's business". Then followed 18 years of obscurity. In the text Jesus is 30 years old. He has been prepared through baptism and the wilderness temptation to preach repentance from sin.

Before this time (vs. 13-16), He had experienced rejection in his hometown of Nazareth; so Capernaum became his headquarters, so to speak. This was also the fulfillment of a prophecy in Isaiah 9:2, "The people that walked in darkness have seen a great light: they that dwell in the land of the shadow of death, upon them hath the light shined." By this time, John the Baptizer had been imprisoned. Heretofore, no Word of redemption had been officially offered to the Gentiles (v. 15); but v. 16 says "...to them .. the light is sprung up."

Jesus' message sounded very much like that of John the Baptist; Matt. 3:2, "...repent ye: for the kingdom of heaven is at hand". The reason these messages sound similar is because they really are alike. These sermons are to alert and alarm; they get your attention, then they prepare you with an in-filling of truth. John 8:32, "...ye shall know the truth, and the truth shall make you free."

Jesus said, "Repent...", recognize the error of your ways. See your life as it really is, not as you suppose it to be. Repent! Do not live in denial, trying to rationalize away your negative thoughts and deeds. Repent! Come to grips with the fact that you are a sinner, and desire to change your life's direction. Repent! Come to experience heartfelt sorrow over the fact that you do sin and displease God. Then ask God to forgive you of those sins, with the express intention of not repeating them. To repent is to relent, and unconditionally surrender to God. It is the spiritual removal of the clothes of sin. Repentance bares the soul for spiritual cleansing. Repentance is one of the elements of conversion leading to a new life, a new relationship with God, through Jesus Christ.

The other element leading to conversion is a belief in the Father's "...only begotten Son...", Jesus Christ. This belief comes by faith, "...for we walk by faith and not by sight". When these two elements are enjoined, things happen. Repentance + Belief = Salvation! Salvation is freedom *FROM* the condemnation (conviction) of sin, which was wrought for us upon the cross of Calvary.

Jesus preached, "Repent, for the kingdom of heaven is at hand". This divine proclamation is only found in the gospel of Matthew because it is the 'Gospel of Jehovah's King'. It is a dispensational phrase which refers to the Messiah's kingdom on earth, offered by both John the Baptist and Jesus (Mt. 3:2; 4:17). When Jesus sent the twelve to evangelize, He commanded in Mt. 10:7, "And as ye go, preach, saying, The kingdom of Heaven is at hand." This kingdom was rejected of men and postponed until Christ comes to set up the His kingdom. Matthew 11:12, "And from the days of John the Baptist until now, the kingdom of heaven suffereth violence, and the violent take it by force."

It is now the time (era) of profession of faith, the dispensation of grace. The parables concerning the kingdom of God (Matthew 13) apply to this age in which we life. At the end of this age, Christ will come and establish a literal earthly kingdom, forever (Mt. 25:31-46; Rev. 11:15; 19:11 - 20:10; Zech. 14; Dan. 2:44-45; Lk. 1:32-33). Within that first millennium (1,000 years) of His eternal reign, He will put down all rebellion, and will rid the earth of all rebellious unbelievers; then Satan, his followers and their deeds shall be put under Jesus' feet forever.

This is our time of preparation. God has given us this opportunity to get ready for the second advent (coming) of Christ. So make good use of your time, because time is definitely winding up. Soon "the trumpet will sound, and the dead in Christ shall rise", and we will see Jesus, the Lion of Judah, coming through the clouds. It is time to repent, for the kingdom of heaven is at hand. Your opportunities may be few, after hearing this message, so do not hesitate to respond. Make your decision to change your eternal destination.

When you repent, you can have that salvation paid for by the blood of Jesus Christ upon the cross. He became the last blood sacrifice for the redemption of man. "By his stripes are ye healed". He died upon Calvary. He was buried in Joseph's new tomb. His Spirit went into Hell, for and won the keys to death, Hell, and the grave. He went back through the grave, picked up that same body; and He rose from the grave on the third day. He is alive forevermore. He is coming back again, so be ready when he comes.

Special Reference Notes

Our New Nature Evidenced by Our New Living Standard

Confession is good for the soul! The word *confession* indicates and implies an action or deed perpetrated against another. There must be a contrite acknowledgment to God of one's sin, in order to receive his full, merciful justification. The Christian is a human, mortal being whose heart has been convicted by the Spirit of God; and because of that event, his spirit has been reworked, refashioned and reshaped. The Christian is a reborn soul, therefore he/she has a new beginning to the relationship with God, through Jesus the Christ. He/She has a new nature, and it can be proved through or by his/her new standard of living.

Jesus alerted, alarmed and allured his followers through his late night conversation with the Jewish leader, Nicodemus in John 3, "...except a man be born again, he cannot see the kingdom of God". He went on to explain to this eager, but ill-informed ruler, "Except a man be born of water and of spirit, he cannot enter into the kingdom of God". The key to this entire discourse is that man must receive a new nature (a new spirit), for "That which is born of flesh is flesh; and that which is born of the Spirit is spirit...ye must be born again."

The new nature of man is not of this world. It is not manufactured by a local factory. It cannot be self-imposed, nor self-induced. It cannot be earned by 'good living'. Its merits come not from man's coffers, and its rewards come not from man's benevolence. Man is born into this newness; not naturally or biologically, but spiritually. This new birth is spiritual. Those who accept Christ Jesus are recipients of his love and grace. Upon the profession of our faith, we receive unearned, unmerited favors of God, through Jesus Christ our Lord, which is called "grace".

The Apostle Paul instructs in Romans 10:9 and 10, "...if thou shalt confess with thy mouth the Lord Jesus, and shalt believe with thine heart that God hath raised him from the dead, thou shalt be saved. For with the heart man believeth unto righteousness; and with the mouth confession is made unto salvation." Mankind's new nature begins with self denial, confession of his transgressions, belief in a new master, and acceptance of the redemptive acts of God through Jesus Christ. "...whosoever shall call upon the name of the Lord shall be saved." "Therefore we are buried with him by baptism into death: that like as Christ was raised up from the dead by the glory of the Father, even so we also should walk in the newness of life". There is more than one aspect of this 'newness'. It permeates the entire life, and lifestyle.

There are some who have repented, are saved, but find themselves in a backsliden condition. Even we who are saved from sin, do occasionally commit some form of sin or ungodliness. King David who was "a man after God's own heart" found himself to be in such a condition. In Psalms 51, David's contrite heart is made evident. He is repenting of his willful sin against man (Uriah) and God. With a broken heart and a fractured spirit David sought forgiveness, and he repented. In verse 10 he said, "Create in me a clean heart, O God; and renew a right spirit within me".

There is no reason to confess sin, if you have never sinned. All David's requests of verses 1 through 9 are useless if he had not needed a washing and cleansing from sin again. Sins of a backslider must also be blotted out, washed, cleansed, acknowledged and purged again. God must show His mercy, be kind to, forgive, and hide His face again from the sins of a backslider; if he is to be restored to God. A new heart must be created, and a right spirit renewed in the backslider again if he is to experience "the joy of his salvation". David recognized this very fact, so he repented of his sin, and was forgiven.

This gives evidence to the fact that God is ready, willing and able to forgive anyone who exhibits a penitent spirit. No matter what tragedy may derail your life, God can right your life and put it back on track. Before God will exercise his divine right of forgiveness, the sinner must come to repentance; then will he discover that "...God is just to forgive our sin".

Special Reference Notes

CHAPTER FIVE:
What Christians Believe About...
BAPTISM

1. What is baptism?

   _____

   _____

   _____

2. Who meets the criteria to be baptized?

   _____

   _____

3. With what three divine personalities are we brought into contact through baptism? (Mt. 28:19)

   (A.)_____

   (B.) _____

   (C.) _____

4. What three great facts of Christ's life on earth do we show forth in baptism? (Rom. 6:4; Col. 2:12)

   (A.)_____

   (B.) _____

   (C.) _____

5. What three acts precede water baptism? (Mk. 16:16; Acts 2:38; 8:37)

   (A.)_____

   _____

   (B.) _____

   _____

   (C.) _____

   _____

6. We should follow Jesus into baptism. (Mk. 1:9; Col. 2:12; Rom. 6:4)

_____

_____

_____

_____

_____

_____

7. Is water baptism essential to salvation?

_____

_____

8. Would the neglect of baptism be in the will of God? (Mt. 3:15-17)

_____

_____

_____

_____

_____

_____

9. Is baptism a proper qualification for local church membership? (Acts 2:41)

_____

_____

_____

_____

10. What is the proper procedure in the implementation of baptism? (Mt. 3:16)

_____

_____

_____

_____

_____

_____

11. Does the Bible support 'sprinkling' as a form of baptism? (circle one)
Yes or No? If so, write the supporting scripture.

_____

_____

12. At the baptism of Jesus, What astounding mystery occurred? (Mt. 3:17)

_____

_____

_____

_____

_____

_____

_____

13. Does the Bible support 'spirit baptism'? (Jn. 3:5-6)

_____

_____

_____

14. By what authority OR in whose name should baptism be performed? (Mt. 28:19-20)

_____

_____

_____

15. Using all of this Holy Bible-based information, answer the following: Is INFANT BAPTISM scriptural? Yes or No? (circle one) Explain!

_____

_____

_____

_____

_____

_____

Special Reference Notes

Three 'Baptisms' for Believers

Baptism must be understood by the believer, and to better understand, I have dissected "Baptism" into three (3) distinct sections.

Baptism One: BAPTISM INTO CHRIST

This is baptism into the body of Christ which occurs at repentance and conversion (Rom. 6:3-7; 1 Cor. 12:13; Gal. 3:27; Col. 2:12). This baptism is at the new birth. Ephesians 4:5 refers to "one baptism" because it is the only baptism that saves the soul of mankind, and adopts the believer into the body of Christ (Jn. 1:12).

Baptism Two: WATER BAPTISM

This particular baptism only takes place after one is saved (after private repentance, and public acknowledgment of that inward conversion) (Rom. 10:9-10).

What is "water baptism"? It is that public act of bodily immersion down into and up out of water which demonstrates or identifies the new convert as a follower of Jesus Christ. This takes place after one is actually saved from sin. This is an act of obedience to the command of our Lord, Jesus Christ.

A. Christian baptism in water... Mt. 28:19; Mk. 16:16; Acts 2:38-41; 8: 12-16, 36-38; 9:18; 10:47-48; 16:15, 38; 18:8; 19:5; 22:16; 1 Cor. 1:13-17; 1 Pe. 3:21

B. Scriptural reasons that forgiveness comes NOT BY WATER...
1. On occasions, confession of sins was required and was made before baptism was performed (Mt. 3:8, 11; Mk. 1:5; Lk. 3:8-14)

2. Only believers were baptized after repentance and faith in Christ (Mt. 28:19; Mk. 16:16; Acts 2:28, 41; 8:12-13, 37;16:14-15, 31-33; 18:8; 19:1-7), and in some cases, after receiving the Holy Spirit (Acts 9:17-18; 10:44-48).

3. Jesus Christ, who knew no sin, was baptized by John the Baptizer (Baptist) in the River Jordan. He submitted to water baptism for two (2) reasons: (1) To fulfill righteousness (Mt. 3:15) and (2) To be manifest to Israel (Jn. 1:31).

4. Water baptism symbolizes the death, burial and resurrection of the Lord, Jesus Christ (1Pe. 3:21). It also represents the death of the old life of the repentant Christian, his/her burial into Jesus Christ, and the resurrection to the new life of the Spirit of God. "If any man be in Christ he is a new creature, old things are passed away, behold all things are become new." (2 Corinthians 5:17)

5. Water Baptism is NOT ESSENTIAL TO SALVATION (1Cor. 1:13-21)

6. Faith in the blood of Jesus Christ brings remission of sin (Mt. 26:28; Rom. 3:24-25, 4:1-25, 5:1-11, 8:2, 10:1-10; 1 Cor. 15:1-5;; Eph. 1:7, 2:8-9; Gal. 3:19-29; Jn. 3:16; Acts 10:43, 13:38-39; 1 Cor. 1:18-21; 1 Jn. 1:9, 5:1)

7. Old Testament saints, as well as John the Baptist and all in Luke 1:15, 41, 46, 67; 2:25-38 who were filled with the Holy Spirit; were saved without water baptism.

8. Jesus Christ forgave (forgives) sin without water baptism (Mt. 9:1-7; Lk. 7:36-50,18:9-14, 19:1-9, 23:43; Jn. 4:49-53, 7:31, 8:30-31, 11:45, 12:11,42; Acts 3:1-11, 16, 4:10-12)

9. Water baptism does not put away (exonerate from, nor absolve of) the filth of the flesh (1 Pe. 3:21)

Baptism Three: BAPTISM OF THE HOLY SPIRIT

The distribution (sanctification) of power for the purpose of service can take place before water baptism (Acts 10:44-48) or after it (Acts 1:4-8, 2:1-11, 8:12-21, 19:1-7). The Holy Spirit is the agent who baptizes INTO CHRIST and INTO HIS BODY (1 Cor. 13:13). Jesus Christ is the agent who baptizes in the Holy Spirit (Mt. 3:11; Jn. 1:31-33) and the minister of the gospel/pastor is the agent who baptizes (immerses) the convert into water (Mt. 28:19).

*NOTE - Please understand that no one can be saved through nor by WATER BAPTISM alone. One can be saved through BAPTISM INTO CHRIST through and by the profession of faith in Christ Jesus, as Redeemer, and by the remission (repentance) of sin.

Baptism is an act of obedience supported by Jesus Christ, and left to the Church as one of two "ordinances". No one is actually saved because he/she experiences water baptism, rather when he/she is saved from sin he/she takes on baptism. So baptism is an outward act of obedience and public acknowledgment of an inward act already experienced. It is an act of endorsement, so to speak.

Jesus was baptized by John the Baptizer (Baptist) in Matthew 3:13-16; and we are to follow His example. We learn by the example given by Jesus that the baptized must be submerged (immersed) into water, and not receive a sprinkling of water upon the head nor a pouring of water over the head. See Matthew 3:16.

The act of baptism should be experienced only by those individuals who have repented of sin, and have confessed a belief in the Son of God, Jesus Christ (Rom. 10:9-10). This is the act of "being born again" spoken of in John 3.

Special Reference Notes

CHAPTER SIX:

What Christians Believe About...

The LORD'S SUPPER

1. What is the Lord's Supper?

_____

_____

_____

_____

_____

_____

2. Who gave us the Lord's Supper? (I Cor. 11:23-26)

_____

_____

_____

_____

3. When and where was it instituted? (Mt. 26:17-30)

_____

_____

_____

_____

4. What particular elements does the Lord's Supper consist of?
   A._____ B. _____

5. What do these two elements represent?

_____

_____

_____

6. Is there anything "spiritual" about these elements? If so, what?

_____

_____

_____

_____

7. Did the early Christians observe the Lord's Supper? If so, how? (Acts 2:42; 20:7)

_____

_____

_____

_____

_____

8. How often should we partake of the Lord's Supper? (Acts 20:7)

_____

_____

_____

9. (Answer YES or NO to the following questions)

    (A) Does this ordinance, the Lord's Supper, save the soul? _____

    (B) Does it absolve sin? _____

    (C) Does it make you a better Christian? How? _____

    (D) Is there any one particular day of the week or the month that we must observe the Lord's Supper? _____

    (E) Are 'Communion' and "The Lord's Supper" the same? _____

10. Why should we continue to observe the Lord's Supper? (I Cor. 11:24-30)

_____

_____

_____

_____

_____

_____

11. Where in the New Testament is the first reference to the ordinance called the "Lord's Supper"? Give the scripture.

_____

12. What names are used in the New Testament for the Lord's Supper? (Acts 2:42; I Cor. 10:16; 11:20; 10:21)

(A) _____

(B) _____

(C) _____

(D) _____

13. From Luke 22:19 we learn the reason we must observe the Lord's Supper. What is that ONE REASON? Because _____!

14. What is meant by not "discerning the Lord's body" in I Cor. 11:29-30?

_____

_____

_____

_____

15. List some things you think about when you partake of the Lord's Supper elements.

_____

_____

_____

_____

_____

_____

_____

_____

_____

_____

_____

_____

_____

OBSERVING THE LORD'S SUPPER

The Lord's Supper
(A Study on Luke 22:1-23)

Verse 1. Beginning with the Passover Feast, the Feast of Unleavened Bread was officially observed. It lasted for seven (7) days. Instructions for this celebration are recorded in Lev. 23:5-8.

> "In the fourteenth day of the Lord, even holy
> convocations , which ye shall proclaim in their seasons.
> And on the fifteenth day of the same month is the
> feast of the unleavened bread unto the Lord: seven days
> ye must eat unleavened bread.
> In the first day ye shall have an holy convocation:
> ye shall do no servile work therein.
> But ye shall offer an offering made by fire unto the
> Lord seven days: in the seventh day is an holy convocation:
> ye shall do no servile work therein."

The 14th of Nisan (April), our Tuesday sunset to Wednesday sunset, the day of the preparation; when the Passover must be killed, the butchering day. The next day would be the 'high day', the great special Sabbath, not the ordinary weekly Sabbath. The regular feast of unleavened bread did not officially begin until a day after the Passover; but Jews began to eat this bread on the day of the preparation.

The two (2) feasts were observed together, because the time for eating the Passover was the commencement of the seven (7) days; during which unleavened bread alone was to be eaten (Ex. 12:1-28; Lev. 23:4-8).

Verse 2... The chief priests and scribes sought how they might turn favorable, popular opinion against Jesus Christ, so that they might safely proceed to kill Him. Or, to kidnap Him, and thus avoid a public trial or hearing. The Greek word for 'kill him' means to take up and carry off. The deal made with Judas Iscariot to deliver Jesus up, was agreed upon the day before Passover began.

Verse 3... Satan, as an angel, could not possibly enter into Judas (bodily that is), for he has his own personal spirit body as big as a man. "The Doctrine of Interpenetration in Scripture, that is, persons entering into each other, as Paul said of Corinthians and Philippians being in his heart (2 Cor. 7:3; Phil. 1:7); God being in Christ (2 Cor. 5:19); Christ being in God (Jn. 14:20) men being in both the Father and the Son (1 Jn. 2:24); etc. It means in union with, consecration to the same end (one mind, purpose and life) not bodily entrance into. Hence, Satan entering into Judas simply means that Judas submitted to Satan's temptation to betray Jesus. So, Judas became one with Satan, like men become one in spirit with God when joined to Him in consecration (1 Cor. 6:17)." (Dake's Annotated Bible Commentary)

Verse 7... refer to verse 1; "Now the feast of unleavened bread drew nigh, which is called the Passover."

Verses 8 - 13... Peter and John, who represented the company of disciples, customarily went to the temple with the Paschal lamb. There, taking turns with others who thronged the temple on the same errand, they killed the lamb, the nearest priest catching the blood in a gold or silver bowl, and passing it on to the next in the row of priests until it reached the one nearest to the altar who instantly sprinkled it toward the altar's base. The lamb was then flayed and the entrails removed, to be burnt with incense on the altar. This was done in the afternoon. When evening came, the lamb was roasted with great care. Unleavened bread, wine, bitter herbs, and sauce were also provided for the supper.

To see a man carrying a pitcher was a rare thing, women usually carried water in pitchers (Gen. 24:14-46; Jn. 4:7). Men usually got water in large skin bottles, and used animals to carry them. Israelites attending the feast at Jerusalem were received by the inhabitants as brothers, and apartments were provided free (with many divans and cushions for many guests to recline on while eating) for them to eat the Passover. In return, the hosts were given the skins of the lambs and the vessels used in the ceremonies.

Verse 14... At sunset the Passover was ready, having been bought, already roasted or prepared beforehand by the disciples, for the regular time for it was not until the next evening. Christ had to partake of it (Passover) a day early, because He was to be on trial all night long , and was to be our Passover sacrifice for us at the regular time on the next afternoon (1Cor. 5:7). Making ready and eating the Passover, in this case, had to be done before the regular time. John tells us (13:1) that it was "before the feast of the Passover" that Christ and His disciples observed the Passover. This was the preparation day, and Jews ate the Passover the next evening. Judas was still one of the twelve.

Verse 16... Proof of the future feast in the eternal kingdom.

Verses 17-18... The Doctrine of the Lord's Supper:

1. It was instituted at the time of the Passover meal (Lk. 22:14-20).
2. It was "the Lord's Supper" (1 Cor. 11:20), and "the communion of the blood of Christ", and the communion of the body of Christ (1 Cor. 10:16).
3. The elements used were "the fruit of the vine" (grape juice of that day, Mk. 14:25, Lk. 22:18) and unleavened "bread" (Mt. 26:17, 26; Mk. 14:12, 22; Lk. 22:7,19).
4. The bread was broken, symbolizing the marred and striped body of Christ for our healing (Mt. 26:26; Lk. 22:19; 1 Cor 10:16; Isa. 52:14; 1 Peter 2:24).
5. The grape juice symbolized the blood of Christ shed for the remission of sin (Mt. 28:28; Mk. 14:24; Lk. 22:20; 1Cor. 11:25-29).
6. Each believer is supposed to partake (Mt. 26:26-27; Mk. 14:22; Lk. 22:17, 19; 1 Cor. 10:16).
7. Thanksgiving and blessings were offered for it (Mt. 26:26-27; Mk. 14:22-23; 1 Cor. 11:24).
8. It is a remembrance of the death of Christ until He comes again (Lk. 22:19; 1 Cor. 11:24-26).
9. It can be partaken daily (Acts 2:42, 46), weekly (Acts 20:7; 1 Cor. 10:17) or as "often" as desired (1Cor. 11:26). Early disciples observed it daily until they began to have weekly meetings, then it was observed every Sunday, according to history and Acts 20:7; 1 Cor. 16:2.
10. It will be observed by Christ and all believers in the Kingdom of God forever (Mt. 26:29; Mk. 14:25; Lk. 22:18, 30)

11. It is an ordinance that should bring unity and love among believers and not division and strife (I Cor. 10:16-17; 11:16-30).

12. It should be partaken in faith and proper examination of self or Lord's Supper condemnation, sickness and even death may result (1 Cor. 11:17-30).

Special Reference Notes

This do in remembrance of me

"And he took bread, and gave thanks, and brake it, and gave unto them, saying, This is my body which is given for you: this do in remembrance of me.

Likewise also the cup after supper, saying, This cup is the new covenant in my blood, which is shed for you". (Luke 22:19-20)

Monuments are erected as special memorials, and serve as reminders of specific people and events, and their unique importance. We are aware of memorials all around our country and the world, i.e.. the Lincoln Memorial, the Jefferson Monument, the eternal flame of former US President John F. Kennedy, the memorial to Martin Luther King, Jr. in Atlanta, Georgia, the Viet Nam War Veterans' Memorial, libraries, bridges, towers and skyscrapers. We erect memorials to remind us of the contribution made to our society.

Since Jesus Christ came to earth to establish his kingdom in the hearts of mankind, it was not necessary to build a physical monument to remember him, or what he had accomplished. Our remembrances of him should be of a more personal and spiritual nature. Our remembrances of him should be in our hearts. However, Jesus did leave us two memorials in the form of ordinances, "BAPTISM and the LORD'S SUPPER".

What must we remember about Jesus? Christians must constantly be mindful of the redemptive acts performed for us by Jesus Christ. When mankind's horrendous relationship with God had no means of rectification, it was Jesus the Christ, God's "only begotten Son" who voluntarily became of hope and salvation.

Jesus "...took bread, and gave thanks, and brake it, and gave unto them, saying, This is my body which is given for you:" (Lk. 22:19). We must remember the bread and what it stands for with regard to our salvation. It is one of the two (2) earthly elements used as a symbol of Christ's sacrificial substitute for sin. The bread was broken symbolizing the marred and striped body of Christ for our spiritual healing. Apostle Paul asked in 1 Cor. 10:16, "This bread which we break, is it not the communion of the body of Christ?" The bread speaks of His body broken because he was made sin for us. His physical bones were not broken during crucifixion, but he was marred due to the magnitude of our sin. "For he hath made him to be sin for us, who knew no sin; that we might be made the righteousness of God in him " (2 Cor. 5:21).

Contrary to the usual crucifixion, Christ's physical body was not broken. The executioners would normally break the legs (bones) of the victim to inflict more pain upon the dying, as well as try to hurry along the impending death. Psalms 34:19-20, "Many are the afflictions of the righteous: but the Lord delivereth him out of them all. He keepeth all this bones: not one of them is broken." The Psalmist was actually prophesying about Christ's coming sacrifice upon Calvary's cross.

What must we remember? Remember the cup, representing Christ's precious blood. Leviticus 17:11 says, "For the life of the flesh is in the blood: and I have given it to you upon the altar to make an atonement for your souls: for it is the blood that maketh an atonement for the soul". Jesus Christ, in Matthew 26:27-28, "...took the cup, and gave thanks, and gave it to them, saying Drink ye all of it: For this is my blood of the new testament, which is shed for many for the remission of sin." The old covenant was dedicated, inaugurated by the blood of animals (Ex. 24:4-8). Hebrews 9:22, "And almost all things are by the law purged with blood: and without shedding of blood is no remission."

That cup containing the "fruit of the vine" was the second earthly element symbolizing the blood of Christ, shed for the remission of sin. The Lord took two (2) of the world's most frail elements, as symbols of his body and blood, bread and wine. Both will spoil in a few days. "...this do in remembrance of me". When he raised a monument, it was not made of brass or marble, brick and mortar, wood nor asphalt. It was not erected upon government grounds. It was made of two frail, perishable elements to be used to remember his sacrifice for the souls of mankind and the remission of sin.

We should remember to take part in the Lord's Supper. "And when he had given thanks, he brake it, and said, Take eat: this is my body, which is broken for you: this do in remembrance of me. After the same manner also he took the cup, when he had supped, saying, This cup is the new testament in my blood: this do ye, as oft as ye drink it, in remembrance of me. For as often as ye eat this bread, and drink this cup, ye do shew the Lord's death till he come." (1 Cor. 11:25-27). Jesus said in Luke 22:16, "I will not any more eat thereof, until it be fulfilled in the kingdom of God."

It is commanded of us, by our Savior, to participate in this act of remembrance - The Lord's Supper. It is also an outward evidence to the world that we are God's people. It announces our obedience to Jesus Christ; and we must obey him. We eat and drink in fellowship with each other here on earth; but one day, on the other side of death, we shall eat and drink anew in the kingdom of God.

Remember what the Lord Jesus had sacrificed to provide everlasting life for all who believe in his name.

Special Reference Notes

CHAPTER SEVEN:
What Christians Believe About…
PRAYER *and* PRAYING

What is PRAYER? It is a mode of spiritual communication between the mortal creature (mankind) and the eternal Creator (God, the Father) through Jesus the Christ. Through or by prayer we supplicate; asking, seeking, pleading and thanking. Prayer is the Christian's greatest ally in every situation, and weapon against trouble and foes.

There are no designed lengths of prayer, nor are there any special words need to orchestrate a specific, pre-determined response. Prayers should always come from the heart. They should not be canned or patented, rather they should be genuine and personal. Though they may be uttered publicly (aloud), they should not be for personal gratification or applause (vanity).

1. Using the numbers 1 - 10, prioritize your reasons for prayer in your personal life!
   ( ) Praying to get something you do not already possess
   ( ) Praying that you may keep something you have
   ( ) Praying to give thanks for your blessings
   ( ) Praying to become more like Christ
   ( ) Praying for the needs of others
   ( ) Praying to become one with the Father
   ( ) Praying for salvation
   ( ) Praying for forgiveness of your sin
   ( ) Praying for your enemies
   ( ) Praying for the Church and her ministry

2. Below find four (4) different types of prayers. In the space provided, define each in your own words.
   a. Prayer of Contrition: _____
   b. Prayer of Supplication: _____
   c. Prayer of Thanksgiving: _____
   d. Prayer of Intercession: _____

3. When you offered *grace* over your last meal, what type of prayer was it? (See above) **A   B   C   D** (Circle One)

4. Give one (1) well-known example (Book, Chapter & Verse) of David's prayer of forgiveness! _____   _____ **:** _____

5. Are we promised that our prayers will be answered? (Mt.7:7-11; 21:22; Mk. 11:24; Jn. 16:23)

   _____

   _____

6. By what conditions does God answer prayers, and fulfill His promises to us?
   a. Jn. 14:13, _____
   b. Mt. 18:19, _____
   c. Jn. 15:7, _____
   d. 1 Jn. 5:14, _____

7. In the prayer life of Jesus, what is the difference in the length of His...

   (A) Private prayers (Lk. 6:12; Mt. 26:36-44; Jn. 17:26), and

   (B) His public prayers (Mt. 11:25-27; Jn. 11:41-42; Lk. 23:34)?

   _____

   _____

   _____

   _____

   _____

8. Should we have both public **AND** private prayers?   **YES**   or **NO**

   (circle one)

9. Are there times when we are expected to stop our praying? If so, when and why?

_____

_____

_____

10. Daniel prayed three times daily. Why? (Dan. 6:10)

_____

_____

_____

_____

_____

11. What was the Jewish system of prayer? What was expected? (**DO YOUR RESEARCH**)

_____

_____

_____

_____

12. What is the "model prayer" most frequently called? (Mt. 6:9-13; Lk. 11:1-11)

_____

_____

_____

_____

13. When the disciples asked Jesus to teach them to pray, what was the lesson? (Mt. 6:9-13)

_____

_____

_____

_____

_____

14. Consider the elements that make up the "Lord's Prayer". (Mt. 6) Each part has special significance.

    a. **A personal relationship with God** ...... "Our Father"   Verse _____

    b. **Faith** .... "which art in heaven"   Verse _____

    c. **Worship** .... "hallowed be thy name"   Verse _____

    d. **Expectation** .... "thy kingdom come"   Verse _____

    e. **Submission** .... "thy will be done in earth, as it is in heaven"   Verse _____

    f. **Petition** .... "give us this day our daily bread"   Verse _____

    g. **Confession** .... "and forgive us our debts"   Verse _____

    h. **Compassion** .... "as we forgive our debtors"   Verse _____

    i. **Dependence** .... "and lead us not into emptation but deliver us from evil"   Verse _____

    j. **Acknowledgment** .... "for thine is the kingdom, and the power, and the glory forever"   Verse _____

15. What promise do you find in this prayer that directly connects YOU to your FELLOWMAN? (Mt. 6:14-15)

_____

_____

_____

16. In whose name, or by what authority do we pray?

_____

(Jn. 14:13-14; 16:26)

17. What 5-letter word must be linked to prayer?

_____ _____ _____ _____ _____ (Heb. 11:6)

18. Analyze the so-called "Lord's Prayer", which should be called the DISCIPLES' PRAYER, because it is the <u>model prayer</u> used by Jesus to teach disciples to pray. What do YOU notice about it? (Mt. 6:9-13)

_____

_____

_____

_____

_____

_____

_____

19. For whom should we pray? (Using the following Scriptures, discover each answer.)

A. Mt. 14:30; Lk. 23:42 _____

_____

B. Jas. 5:16; Rom. 1:9 _____

_____

C. Eph. 6:19-20; Col. 4:3 _____

_____

_____

D. Jas. 5:14-15 _____

_____

_____

E. 1 Tim. 2:1-3 _____

_____

_____

F. Mt. 5:44; Lk. 6:28 _____

_____

Special Reference Notes

A Praying Activity

Instructions: Using the previous information about prayer, in this chapter, write a prayer expressing your repentance for past sins. Be honest, earnest, clear and concise. Remember who you are talking to.

_____

_____

_____

_____

_____

_____

_____

_____

_____

_____

_____

_____

_____

_____

_____

_____

_____

_____

_____

_____

_____

_____

_____

_____

_____

_____

A Lesson On Prayer

"Thy kingdom come. Thy will be done in earth, as it is in heaven."
(Mt. 6:10)

Prayer, for the Christian, is an absolute necessity. It shows obedience to God, who insists that we do pray to Him. In Luke 11:1, Jesus' disciples said, "...Lord, teach us to pray, as John also taught his disciples". The disciples had been with Jesus, and had come to know that His prayers were always heard and answered. They discovered that the continual source of his power and utter freedom from pride came through secret prayer. Jesus gave a model for our praying ("The Lord's Prayer") which contained 23 elements, of which four will be used for this treatise... **Anticipation, Consecration, Universality and Conformity** This prayer lesson began by establishing a proper relationship with the deity by saying "Our Father...". Then came the element of proper recognition; "...which art in heaven". The element which followed was adoration; "hallowed be thy name".

The next four elements are the focus of this lesson text. ANTICIPATION; "Thy kingdom come". The true Christian lives in hope for God's kingdom to actually come; this of course refers to Christ's second advent (coming). Our lives here on earth are to prepare for His coming. Zechariah 14 clearly describes events that shall occur which signify the second coming, and its repercussions. Then in Rev. 11:15, "The kingdoms of this world are become the kingdoms of our Lord, and of his Christ; and he shall reign for ever and ever." This prophetic announcement will actually be fulfilled after the three and a half years of Rev. 19:11-21. The casting out of Satan from heaven under the 7th trumpet makes it possible for God to take over the governments of this world. At the time He has planned to do so, then will come the second advent. With this acquired knowledge we must live for, desire and pray for God's kingdom to come.

Our only problem with this statement is making sure that we are prepared for it, whenever it does actually come. Our anticipation must be undergirted with preparation. Surely no one wants Jesus to return to find the same person as before conversion; being envious, full of malice, evil speaking, ungodly, hateful, stingy, uncaring, unkind, stiff-necked and full of pride, so you have been given this time to prepare through prayer and supplication and by works for Christ's coming. **"Our Father, which art in heaven. Thy kingdom come..."**

Jesus then taught **"thy will be done"**, which is the element of CONSECRATION. This was not merely an act of doing, but it was also an attitude; the attitude that Jesus possessed. He desired to be of use to God the Father, so the work he did was by the will of God. Jesus was the incarnate God, but while he was clothed in the flesh he sought God to direct his life. Now if Jesus (being human and divine) could see the necessity of having God to direct HIS life, what about the lives of all human kind? What about YOUR life? Do you seek to know God's will before you take action? When you consecrate your life to God, when you say **"thy will be done"** you are surrendering to God's express will. Jesus himself declared, "I came to do the will of my Father". To consecrate is to prepare, through prayer, to accomplish a task, a work for the Lord.

"In earth" refers to God's UNIVERSALITY. We are aware of the three realms; Heaven, Earth and Hell. Physically, we live in the realm called Earth, but we have the hope of going to live, spiritually, in the realm called Heaven. Unfortunately, those who never accept Jesus Christ as Saviour and Lord will live in the eternally destructive realm called Hell. The phrase "in earth" deals with God's omnipresence, his ability to be everywhere at the same time.

God desires that his will be executed everywhere on the earth, so Christians must learn to live within his divine will. Christians exist to please God. We are here on earth as agents, ambassadors of the risen Saviour to do his will. God desires his Word to become universal, so mankind, from the four corners of the earth can be saved "in earth".

"as it is in heaven" - CONFORMITY...to bring into likeness or oneness; to make the same. In this, heaven and earth are in relationship with each other. God desires to have serenity, bliss of the pre-Adamic covenant. God desires oneness amongst mankind and between God and man. That is why John 3:17 is so important..."For God sent not his Son into the world to condemn the world, but that the world through him might be saved." God wants a re-uniting of heaven and earth. He wants to develop a new relationship with mankind, one based upon his Son Jesus Christ. God wants these earthly time travelers to conform to heavenly principles and practices. The old Negro spiritual declared - "I wanna go to heaven when I die; Good Lord, when I die".

Heaven is not merely a topic of conversation. Heaven is a reality. Heaven is a real geographic location that the physical cannot reach. It is a certainty that the physical (mortal) body returns to the dust from which it came; but the soul goes back to the Lord who gave it. This relationship with God through Jesus Christ is immediate, so we can experience some heaven right here on earth. Anyone who seeks the Lord and determines to live by the commands of Jesus Christ will receive the joy of salvation right here on earth. Jesus prayed, **"Thy kingdom come. Thy will be done in earth**, as it is in heaven "-ANTICIPATION, CONSECRATION, and UNIVERSAL, CONFORMITY to God through Jesus Christ, our Lord.

Special Reference Notes

CHAPTER EIGHT:
What Christians Believe About...
FAITH

1. In what book of the Bible do we find the "Faith Chapter"?

   _____

   _____

2. Identify that chapter by number!

   _____

   _____

3. Using Heb. 11:1, what is Paul's spiritual definition of "FAITH"?

   _____

   _____

   _____

4. How does faith impact our man-God relationship? (Heb. 11:6)

   _____

   _____

   _____

   _____

5. What do you think faith is?

   _____

   _____

   _____

   _____

   _____

   _____

6. Why do we need faith? (Heb. 11:6)

_____

_____

_____

_____

7. Who is the author of this epistle (letter)?

_____

_____

_____

8. Is faith essential to salvation? Yes or No   (circle one)

9. Apostle James teaches us that "faith without _____ is dead". Give the
   scripture, _____. This means that we must animate
   or enliven our faith.

10. Faith is a gift of the Trinity, the Godhead.

   A. Faith is the Gift of the Father; Romans 12:3,
      " _____ "

   B. Faith is a Gift of God, the Son; Hebrews 12:2,
      " _____ "

   C. Faith is the Gift of God, the Holy Spirit; Galatians 5:22,
      " _____ "

11. "For I am not ashamed of the _____ of
    _____; for it is the power of God unto _____ to
    everyone; to the Jew first, and also to the Greek. (Rom. 1:16)

12. "For therein is the righteousness of God revealed from _____ to
    : as it is written, _____.

    (Rom. 1:17; Hab. 2:4)

13. (2 Cor. 5:7)

_____

_____

_____

14. Who was martyred by stoning to death, as he showed great faith? (Acts 7)

_____

_____

_____

15. (Heb. 12:2) "Jesus is the _____ and _____ of the _____."

Stand On Your Faith

"Cast not away therefore your confidence, which hath great recompense of reward.

For ye have need of patience, that, after ye have done the will of God, ye might receive the promise.

For yet a little while, and he that shall come will come, and will not tarry.

Now the just shall live by faith: but if *any man* draw back, my soul shall have no pleasure in him.

But we are not of them who draw back unto perdition; but of them that believe to the saving of the soul." . (Hebrews 10:35-39)

Faith is the base, the foundation of Christianity. We believe the Word of God by our faith in Jesus Christ. Our faith produces works, and our belief is substantiated by the evidence of our works. So, our faith must produce works. We function from a place of faith. Apostle Paul wrote "the just shall live by faith". Apostle James said "faith without works is dead". Amid this perverse generation of lures and temptations, it is easy to be drawn away from the Lord. Our goal is to encourage you to "Stand On Your Faith"; regardless of the outcome.

Hebrews 10:1-6, "For the law having a shadow of good things to come, *and* not the very image of the things, can never with those sacrifices which they offered year by year continually make the comers thereunto perfect.

2 For then would they not have ceased to be offered? because that the worshippers once purged should have had no more conscience of sins.

3 But in those *sacrifices there is* a remembrance again *made* of sins every year.

4 For *it is* not possible that the blood of bulls and of goats should take away sins.

5 Wherefore when he cometh into the world, he saith, Sacrifice and offering thou wouldest not, but a body hast thou prepared me:

6 In burnt offerings and *sacrifices* for sin thou hast had no pleasure." This deals with the effects of the old sacrifices. Before Jesus came to earth, the objects of sacrifices were animals, ie. lambs, rams and doves. Under that system, God made blood the atoning agent.

Paul clarified that God determined that animal sacrifices became insufficient to atone for the mess that man made of his relationship with God. In verse 6, it directly links to John 3:16 and 17, "For God so loved the world that he gave his only begotten Son, that whosoever believeth on him shall not perish, but shall have everlasting life. For God sent not his Son into the world to condemn the world, but that through him the world might be saved."

Jesus sought to take care of the problem of sacrifices and atonement once and for all times, by his own works.

7 "Then said I, Lo, I come (in the volume of the book it is written of me,) to do thy will, O God.

8 Above when he said, Sacrifice and offering and burnt offerings and offering for sin thou wouldest not, neither hadst pleasure therein; which are offered by the law;"

9 Then said he, Lo, I come to do thy will, O God. He taketh away the first, that he may establish the second.

10 By the which will we are sanctified through the offering of the body of Jesus Christ once for all.

11 And every priest standeth daily ministering and offering oftentimes the same sacrifices, which can never take away sins: It was a job well done.

12 But this man, after he had offered one sacrifice for sins for ever, sat down on the right hand of God; (Jesus Christ).

This is the NEW COVENANT (contract) between God and Man! Verse 16 This *is* the covenant that I will make with them after those days, saith the Lord, I will put my laws into their hearts, and in their minds will I write them; 17 And their sins and iniquities will I remember no more.

23 Let us hold fast the profession of *our* faith without wavering; (for he *is* faithful that promised);

24 And let us consider one another to provoke unto love and to good works:

25 Not forsaking the assembling of ourselves together, as the manner of some *is*; but exhorting *one another*: and so much the more, as ye see the day approaching.

26 For if we sin willfully after that we have received the knowledge of the truth, there remaineth no more sacrifice for sins,

27 But a certain fearful looking for of judgment and fiery indignation, which shall devour the adversaries.

28 He that despised Moses' law died without mercy under two or three witnesses:

29 Of how much sorer punishment, suppose ye, shall he be thought worthy, who hath trodden under foot the Son of God, and hath counted the blood of the covenant, wherewith he was sanctified, an unholy thing, and hath done despite unto the Spirit of grace?

Under Moses, the Law could readily point at sin without thought of mercy and grace. Under Jesus, we are taught by precept and example to forgive the sinner or the transgressor. Moses represented the Law, while Jesus represented Mercy. The Law said "You are guilty". Jesus said, I am your justification. Stand On Your Faith, verses 35-39 tell us "Cast not away therefore your confidence, which hath great recompense of reward. For ye have need of patience, that, after ye have done the will of God, ye might receive the promise. For yet a little while, and he that shall come will come, and will not tarry. Now the just shall live by faith: but if *any man* draw back, my soul shall have no pleasure in him. But we are not of them who draw back unto perdition; but of them that believe to the saving of the soul. "By faith are you saved through grace..."

Don't let anything turn you around, but keep your eye on the prize; for there is a crown of righteousness awaiting the faithful. Paul said in 2 Timothy 4:8, "... there is laid up for me a crown of righteousness, which the Lord, the righteous judge, shall give me at that day: and not to me only, but unto all them also that love his appearing."

Special Reference Notes

Walking in Faith

"Therefore we are always confident, knowing, that, while we are at home in the body, we are absent from the Lord: For we walk by faith, not by sight: We are confident, I say, and willing rather to be absent from the body, and to be present with the Lord." (2 Corinthians 5:6-8)

Many people outside of Christ would love to possess a confidence that supersedes mere hope, luck or happenstance. Christians have such a confidence; we call it FAITH. Hebrews 11, verse 1 defines faith on this wise..."Now faith is the substance of things hoped for, the evidence of things not seen. For by it the elders obtained a good report."

The saved have received salvation by faith. Apostle Paul explained this to the Christian at Rome (Rom. 1:17); "The just shall live by faith". This is a quotation from Habakkuk. 2:4, and simply means that the redeemed, the saved, must live by continued faith; and go from faith to faith as light is received. 1 John 1:7 declares, "... if we walk in the light, as he is in the light, we have fellowship one with another, and the blood of Jesus Christ his Son cleanse us from all sin". Verse nine assures "If we confess our sins, he is faithful and just to forgive us our sins, and to cleanse us from all unrighteousness".

Life has a way of lulling us into a sleep of apathy and complacency. Education, money, worldly position and prestige are external attributes looked for by mankind. "Satan desires to sift you as wheat"; but you have hope. God has given his very best for us all. He has prepared a system of salvation for the souls of mankind. He has spiritual help and guidance for your entire life, here and in the life to come. "For God so loved the world that he gave his only begotten Son, that whosoever believeth on him should not perish, but have everlasting life". When one actively accepts God's Gift, it must be done by and through FAITH. It is not based upon worldly things. It cannot be discerned through our senses. It cannot be distinguished by the touch, the ear, the eye, nor the nose. Apostle Paul said, "...we walk by faith, not by sight." The only way to determine whether or not someone is saved by Jesus Christ, is by his faith-walk or his living.

Life on earth is temporary! Some people live as though they are not concerned about what the future has in store. Others believe that God holds their future until judgment. The saved have no problem regarding the future. When this life has been served to its fullest; and time has been called to a sudden halt, and sickness will no longer rule this body, hardships of this life are no more; then our greatest hope is to live with the Lord.

"For we know that if our earthly house of this tabernacle were dissolved, we have a building of God, an house not made with hands, eternal in the heavens." If you believe in Jesus Christ and his acts of redemption on your behalf, and walk by faith; then he will reward you. Heaven shall be your eternal home.

"Without faith it is impossible to please God". God rewards the faithful. Hebrews 11 -

"Abel offered unto God a more excellent sacrifice than Cain..."

"Noah...prepared an ark to the saving of his house...and became heirs of the righteousness which is by faith."

Enoch (who walked with God) was translated that he should not see death... because he pleased God."

"Abraham, sojourned in the land of promise...For he looked for a city which hath foundation, whose builder and maker is God".

Jesus Christ died to prepare a place for all who would believe and have faith in him. He assured the disciples in John 14:1-2, "Let not your hearts be troubled: ye believe in God, believe also in me. In my Father's house are many mansions: if it were not so, I would have told you. I go to prepare a place for you." Then Jesus went to Calvary to purchase our pardons with his own blood. He commended his spirit into God's hands, and gave up the ghost. Jesus died! His body was buried in a borrowed grave, then on the third day morning, Jesus rose from the dead; and He is alive forever. The psalmist wrote...

"My faith looks up to Thee,
Thou Lamb of Calvary,
Savior divine!
Now hear me while I pray,
Take all my guilt away,
O let me from this day
Be wholly Thine!"
-- Ray Palmer

Special Reference Notes

CHAPTER NINE:
What Christians Believe About…

GIVING

1. What is "stewardship"?

   _____

   _____

   _____

   _____

2. Under the Jewish Dispensation, how was religious work supported?
   (Lev. 27:30-33)

   _____

   _____

   _____

   _____

3. What are the two biblical forms of giving?

   _____ & _____

4. What is the "Tithe"? (Lev. 21-22)

   _____

   _____

   _____

   _____

5. What are "Offerings"?

   _____

   _____

   _____

   _____

6. God's system of 'offerings' began in the Old Testament. Below is a list of Scriptures which describe different types of offerings. Using these texts, **name the types of offerings.**

a. _____   Ex. 29:18

b. _____   Lev. 23:13

c. _____   Lev. 7:14

d. _____   Lev. 2:1

e. _____   Lev. 7:11

f. _____   Lev. 4:3

g. _____   Lev. 5:6

h. _____   Lev. 7:30

7. What do tithes and offerings support?

_____

_____

_____

_____

_____

8. What sin do we commit when we withhold tithes and offerings from God? (Mal. 3:8-10)

_____

_____

_____

_____

_____

9. Who was indicted in these scriptures? (Mal. 3)

_____

_____

_____

_____

10. What was the penalty for such actions? (Mal. 3)

_____

_____

_____

_____

11. Complete the following -- "The Lord loveth a cheerful _____".
Now using your Bible concordance, locate this Scripture and record it here: _____

12. Does the New Testament support tithes and offerings? (circle one) YES or NO. If yes, what is the Christian's responsibility? (1 Cor. 16:2)

_____
_____
_____
_____
_____
_____

13. Circle TRUE or FALSE to the following statements OPPOSED 1 Corinthians 16:2.
   a. We should give only when the cause appeals to us   T   F
   b. We should have a regular system of giving   T   F
   c. We should depend upon bake sales, dinners, etc., for the support of the Church   T   F
   d. Everyone should give the same amount, every Sunday   T   F
   e. The amount we give should depend upon our prosperity   T   F
   f. Members should pay DUES to the Church, like those paid to social clubs, fraternities sororities and lodges   T   F
   g. Our gifts should be presented every Saturday (Sabbath)   T   F

14. Does Jesus' teachings support the tithe and offerings system?
   YES or NO (circle one) If YES, find one (1) supporting scripture in your Bible:

_____
_____

15. The "TENTH" : Whose is it?

_____
_____

16. The following is a chart to clarify the "Tenth" (tithe): To use this chart effectively, you must understand the principle of the tenth. **Note:** God, the Father instituted the tithe for the priests (Levites), because this priestly

order was assigned to Temple dwelling and work. Everyone else had a living and could work; but the priests lived and worked at the Temple. God provided for them from the tithes and offerings brought to the Temple. Our present day ministry should be provided for from the tithes and offerings brought to the Church.

To accurately determine your specific tithe, move the decimal (dot or point) one numerical place to the left and that will be a tenth. **EXAMPLE:** If your gross earnings on your check are **$1, 2 3 7 . 1 8,** merely move the decimal one place to the left, and your tithe is... **$123.72**

If your gross earnings are:		Your Tithe is:
$ 50.00	....	$ 5.00
75.00	....	7.50
100.00	....	10.00
150.00	....	15.00
200.00	....	20.00
225.00	....	22.50
250.00	....	25.00
275.00	....	27.50
300.00	....	30.00
350.00	....	35.00
500.00	....	50.00
750.00	....	75.00
1,000.00	....	100.00
1,500.00	....	150.00

17. What about the Offering? How much should I give? How blessed am I?

_____

_____

_____

_____

_____

_____

18. Some reasons for giving money through the Church are...

   A. The Support of God's Work (1 Tim. 5:17-18)

   _____

   _____

   _____

   B. The Receipt of Blessings (Prov. 3:9-10; 28:20; Mal. 3:10; Lk. 6:38; 2 Cor. 9:6)

   _____

   _____

   _____

   C. To Challenge Other Christians (2 Cor. 9:2)

   _____

   _____

   _____

   D. To Glorify God, the Father (2 Cor. 9:12)

   _____

   _____

   _____

   E. To Provide For Needy Saints (Acts 11:29; 1 Jn. 3:17)

   _____

   _____

   _____

   _____

   _____

19. Contributions should also be made as God prospers you. (**A.** 1 Cor. 16:2; **B.** Mal. 3:8; **C.** 2 Cor 8:7)

   _____

   _____

   _____

   _____

   _____

   _____

Special Reference Notes

CHAPTER TEN:
What Christians Believe About...
The RESURRECTION

1. What is the "RESURRECTION"?

   _____

   _____

2. According to Matthew 22:23, who says there is no resurrection?

   _____

   _____

3. What did Jesus say about the resurrection (Jn. 11:25)

   _____

   _____

   _____

   _____

4. Would God's plan of salvation be complete WITHOUT the resurrection?
   Y   N   (circle one) (Explain)

   _____

   _____

   _____

5. As Christians, we believe that our end is to live with the Lord, and we are promised this by Jesus Christ (John 14: 1-2). What did Jesus tell his disciples?

   _____

   _____

   _____

   _____

6. In John 11, Jesus raised _____ from the dead.

7. He is not _____, but is risen: remember how he spake unto you when he was yet in _____," (Luke 24:5)

8. 1Corinthians 15:3-4 states,

"_____

_____

_____ "

9. Jesus said, "I am the _____ and the life: he that be _____ in me, though he were dead, yet shall he live". (Jn. 11:25).

10.Jesus raised _____ from the dead, whom lived in the city of _____ with his 2 sisters.

11.Jesus died upon the cross at _____ , but he rose on the _____ day morning.

12. On resurrection morning, Matthew 28:2 says, "And, behold, there was a _____ : for the _____ of the Lord descended from _____ , and came and rolled back the _____ from the door, and sat upon it".

13."And Jesus came and spake unto them, saying, (Matt. 28:18)

_____

_____

_____

_____

_____

_____

_____

_____

_____

_____

_____

_____

Results of Christ's Resurrection
"Book of Bible LISTS" (p.169)

a. It guarantees our justification   Rom. 4:24

b. It guarantees present-day power and strength   Eph. 1:18-2:10

c. It guarantees fruitful labor   1 Cor. 15:58

d. It guarantees our own resurrection   2 Cor. 4:14

e. It will exchange bodily corruption for incorruption   1 Cor. 15:42

f. It will exchange dishonor for glory   1 Cor 15:43

g. It will exchange our physical weaknesses for power   1 Cor. 15:43

h. It will exchange a material body for a spiritual body   1 Cor. 15:44

i. It emphasizes the deity of Christ   Acts 10:40;
                                                                Rom. 1:4

j. It is the springboard of Christ's exaltation   Acts 5:30-31;
                                                                Phil. 2:9-11

k. It marks the beginning of his lordship over the Church   Eph. 1:19-23

l. It warns the sinner of the coming Judgment Day   Acts 17:31

m. It forever seals the doom of Satan   Heb. 2:14;
                                                                Rev. 20:10

n. It transfers the worship day from Saturday to Sunday   Acts 20:7;
                                                                1Cor. 16:2

He Is Risen, As He Said!

"He is not here: for he is risen, as he said,
Come see the place where the Lord lay." (Matthew 28:6)

Matthew 28:1, "...as it began to dawn..."
Mark 16:2, "And very early in the morning..."
Luke 24:1, "...very early in the morning..."
John 20:1, "...early, when it was yet dark..."

All of the gospel writers agree as to the day and time of the Lord's resurrection. We learn from them that Jesus arose early, before daybreak, at the end of the regular weekly sabbath day. It was three days and nights after the crucifixion at Calvary; today it is celebrated on Sunday morning.

The Resurrection of Christ was Inevitable

Nothing could prevent the resurrection from taking place at the appointed, time and location. No power on earth could prevent it. Even though this tomb was sealed by Roman orders, and guards were changed every 3 hours; and a cord was stretched across the gigantic stone blocking the entrance with an official Roman seal at each end. The resurrection of Jesus had to take place at the specified time.

Pilate's hand washing, the jeering mob crying "Crucify him", Peter's denial, Judas' betrayal; all of these events played their roles in God's plan of salvation, and the resurrection of Jesus Christ. Although Jesus had repeatedly tried to impress upon his disciples that the Messiah would suffer and die before he attained glory, they could not understand. He explained that though he would leave them for a while, he would return from the dead (John 14:1-3). Though the disciples had witnessed Jesus raised the dead, they did not believe that he could conquer his own death.

According to the Jewish establishment and his own disciples, Jesus had not fulfilled the messianic promises. The disciples did not expect to see Jesus again after his death on Calvary, and his subsequent burial in Joseph's new tomb. The women appeared at the tomb, because it was the custom to complete burial preparation. Most of the disciples had gone back to fishing, while the others were hiding for fear of physical harm and death. The tragic events of Jesus' arrest, trial and crucifixion had occurred in such rapid succession that some of the disciples could not even believe that the Lord had died. They were shocked, mystified and heartbroken at the sudden, apparent end of the One they expected to live and reign forever. Jesus gave them a few assurances which seemed to be vague promises; but even these brought a measure of consolation to these bereft followers.

The Resurrection of Christ was Triumphant

The disciples began to ponder over Christ's words. The three years of continuous teaching that the kingdom would be a kingdom of the Spirit, had left little impression on their minds. They coveted earthly gain because they had left all to follow him. They expected to become rulers, governors and judges over an earthly kingdom. These dreams and aspirations soon vanished and their minds were free to contemplate the kingdom. The "Suffering Servant" of Isaiah was the new picture they had of Jesus.

Jesus triumphed over physical forces and death (the enemy of mankind), which can only destroy physical man. He rose with a spiritual body...the new Adam; free from all weakness and limitations which bind the body. His body was transfigured. Now, he could pass through a closed door or move to another location without any hindrance. He has victoriously risen from the grave with a glorious body.

Jesus' disciples and followers who saw him after his resurrection had also risen to a new power. What for a time seemed a dismal failure, turned out to be a triumphant victory. The Master's death had aroused general sympathy and won many followers. That single local event had taken on a global significance. By remaining loyal to him, their fondest dreams would come true. They would sit on "his right hand and on his left" in the new realm; which would conquer all the kingdoms of the earth.

The Resurrection of Christ was Spiritual Vindication

They learned that life on earth is temporal. Life here is preparation for the life to come, and death seemed to take on a new meaning. To the Jews, death was a calamity. To the disciples it was disaster, but it came to mean victory. The physical body of our Lord had died, but his divinity survived. Our Lord had delivered death a mortal blow, and gave immortality a new meaning. John 14:1, "Let not your heart be troubled, ye believe in God believe also in me. In my father's house there are many mansions; if it were not so I would have told you. I go to prepare a place for you that where I am, there you my be also". There is another side to life. We are given this time to prepare for the other side. On this is mortality. On the other side, immortality. On this side is corruption. On the other side incorruption. On this side we shed briny tears, On the other side, God shall wipe every tear from our eyes. On this side is sorrow. On the other side is joy. On this side we experience loss. On the other side there is eternal gain. On this side is a warfare. On the other side is victory.

When Christ, the Redeemer, rose from the dead, there was another earthquake; the second one in three days. "The angel of the Lord descended from heaven and rolled back the stone from the door, and sat there on". On other occasions angels appeared like men, without such an overt display of power. But verse 3 says, "His countenance was like lightning, and his raiment white as snow." This kind of appearance demonstrated by what power the stone had been rolled away. The angel answered the women's stifling fear in verses 5 and 6, "Do not fear, I know you are looking for Jesus who was crucified. He is not here: for he is risen, as he said. Come see the place where the Lord was buried".

Let us take a look back over time to put things in order. Only thirty-three years earlier, on a hillside in Galilee the angelic host announced a miraculous event, which began the work of salvation. They heralded the good news..."Unto you is born this day in the city of David, the Saviour which is Christ the Lord". But now, on this new day, God dispatched his angelic ambassador to testify to the validity of Christ's resurrection. "He is not here, for he has risen as he said. Go tell my disciples to meet him in Galilee."

Today you need to go and tell somebody about the Lord, Jesus Christ! Evangelize your home, your job, your neighborhood. Testify to the glory of the Lord. Share the goodness of God through Jesus Christ. Tell everybody that you know about Jesus. **Tell Them That...**

-- Jesus is God's only begotten Son
-- Jesus died upon Calvary for the sins of mankind
-- He was wounded for you and me

- He was placed in Joseph's new tomb
- Early on the 3rd day morning he rose to life again
- He was seen going away in a cloud
- He is coming back again
- He loves everybody, and wants them to be saved
- He will forgive their sins, their errors, their mistakes
- Jesus is the Saviour of the world.

Special Reference Notes

CHAPTER ELEVEN:

What Christians Believe About…

the Work of the HOLY SPIRIT in the New Testament

1. Who is the Holy Spirit?

   _____

   _____

2. What person of the divine Trinity (the Godhead) does the Holy Spirit hold?

   _____

   _____

   _____

   _____

3. Is the Holy Spirit a personality or a force? (Jn. 14:16-17)

   _____

   _____

   _____

   _____

4. The first mention of the Holy Spirit comes early in the Bible? (Gen. 1:2) What does it say?

   _____

   _____

   _____

   _____

   _____

   _____

5. Give another New Testament name for the Holy Spirit used by Jesus Christ. (Jn. 14:16)

_____

_____

6. Is the Holy Spirit at work today, as in apostolic times? (Acts 2)

_____

_____

_____

_____

7. What is the work of the Holy Spirit? SCRIPTURE?

_____

_____

_____

_____

_____

8. Is mankind in control of the Holy Spirit, or is the Holy Spirit in control of mankind? Does He do what you want, when you want, just because you want him to? Explain!

_____

_____

_____

_____

9. Is the Holy Spirit essential to the Christian? How?

_____

_____

_____

_____

10.What is the fruit of the Spirit in our lives? (Gal. 5:22-24)

_____

_____

_____

_____

11. What is that unmistakable evidence of salvation? (1 Jn. 3:14)

_____

_____

_____

_____

_____

12. The disciples were instructed by Jesus to go to Jerusalem to wait for the promise (Acts 1:8). At our conversion the Holy Spirit becomes manifest in the life of the believer. Is it necessary now to 'tarry' (wait) for His presence in this dispensation (time) of Grace? Explain!

_____

_____

_____

_____

_____

_____

13. Are the names 'Holy Spirit' and 'Holy Ghost' the same?
    YES or **NO** (circle one)

14. Is the Holy Spirit a 'feeling' managed by the five senses of humanity?
    YES or **NO** (circle one)

15. Can manifestations of the Holy Spirit be controlled by mankind? EXPLAIN!

_____

_____

_____

_____

_____

_____

7. "...It is expedient for you that I go away: for if I go not away, the Comforter will not come unto you; but if I depart, I will send him unto you.

8. And when he is come, he will reprove the world of sin. and of righteousness, and of judgment:

9. Of sin, because they believe not on me;

10. Of righteousness, because I go to my Father, and ye see me no more;

11. Of judgment, because the prince of this world is judged.

12. I have many things to say unto you, but ye cannot bear them now.

13. Howbeit when he, the Spirit of truth, is come, he will guide you into all truth: for he shall not speak of himself; but whatsoever he shall hear, that shall he speak: and he will shew you things to come.

14. He shall glorify me: for he shall receive of mine, and shall shew it unto you." (John 16:7-14)

Since believers is born again (anew) (Jn. 3:1-13) through Jesus Christ, and are the recipients of the Holy Spirit; we should certainly know and somewhat understand what He does on our behalf. The Holy Spirit has a definite duty, purpose and responsibility.

The Holy Spirit establishes our relationship with God, the Father. Salvation is that experience by which we are brought back into fellowship with God. By its conviction of our sin(s) is removed by the cleansing blood of the Lamb of God, Jesus Christ; spiritual barriers are broken down, obstacles are swept away, and we are reconciled back to God. Second Corinthians 5:19 declares "...God was in Christ reconciling the world to himself, not imputing their trespasses unto them; and hath committed unto us the word of reconciliation". Apart from Christ there can be no relationship with God. Some think it is to possible believe in God without a belief in Jesus Christ (God's Son), but they do not understand the Trinity, nor its function. The divine Trinity is the triune-God: God in three personalities (Three-In-One), God the Father, God the Son, God the Holy Ghost. the Father creates, the Son redeems (saves from sin), and the Holy Spirit keeps (maintains). Jesus Christ declared, "I am the way, the truth and the life: no man cometh unto the Father, but by me" (Jn. 14:6). This scripture should clear away mankind's confusion as to whether to accept Jesus Christ as Savior or not. "...no man cometh to the Father but by me." Jesus opened the door, and the Holy Spirit confirms mankind's relationship with God Almighty.

The Holy Spirit enriches the lives of believers. He dwells within the life of all Christ-believers to help (assist) in experiencing the abundant life that Jesus Christ provides. He enriches the believers' lives by giving useful gifts. First Corinthians 12:7, "...the manifestation of the Spirit is given to every man to profit withal". He enriches the believers' lives by producing certain fruits within them. Galatians 5:22-23, "The fruit of the Spirit is love, joy, peace, longsuffering, gentleness, goodness, faith, meekness, temperance: against such there is no law." He enriches the believers' lives by developing them toward Christ-likeness according to Ephesians 1:13-14, "In whom ye also trusted, after that ye heard the word of truth, the gospel of your salvation: in whom also after that ye believed, ye were sealed with that Holy Spirit of promise; which is the earnest of our inheritance until the redemption of the purchased possession, unto the praise of his glory".

The Holy Spirit enriches the mind of the believer. John 16:12-13, "I have yet many things to say unto you, but ye cannot bear them now. Howbeit when he, the Spirit of truth, is come, he will guide you into all truths: for he shall not speak of himself; but whatsoever he shall hear, that shall he speak: and he will shew you things to come". The disciples did not have the ability to fully understand all the words of Jesus, though they were with him in person for three and a half years. Even today we do not have that ability, and that is where the Holy Spirit enters. He provides clarity to the words of Jesus Christ for and to the believer. He interprets the Word of God to us, for our greater understanding. When we understand God's Word, we are more likely to please Him by following (doing) his commands. The Bible contains innumerable mysteries which confound, confuse and baffle the finite minds of mankind. It is within the parameters of the Holy Spirit to provide adequate interpretation, thus providing understanding (clarity) to the Word.

He enriches the believers' lives by encouraging their hearts. In our stress conscious society, depressions and discouragement are familiar companions.

Illness, family and social problems, and a myriad of disappointments cause feelings of discouragement. The promise of Jesus Christ is that whenever discouragement and depressions set in, the Holy Spirit is not merely with us, but He is also within us to provide consolation. He is there when things do not seem to go the way we intend. The Holy Spirit helps us to stay focused on the mark, and always leads "...into the paths of righteousness".

The Holy Spirit empowers the spirit of the believer. In preparation for service, our Lord instructed the his disciples to return to Jerusalem. They were to wait to "be endued with power from on high". In Acts 1:8 Jesus said, "But ye shall receive power, after that the Holy Ghost is come upon you: and ye shall be witnesses unto me both in Jerusalem, and in Judaea, and in Samaria, and unto the uttermost part of the earth". The believer is saved from sin and acts of sin. He is saved from eternal destruction, from moral decay and all that detracts from godliness. The believer is saved to do the will of the Father as guided by the Holy Spirit. He is saved to live the righteous life as prescribed by Jesus Christ, the Lord. This being the case, the Holy Spirit performs the works orchestrated by God. This empowers the believer to function within the expressed will of God.

No work for Christ can be effectively performed until His Spirit has prepared, fortified and empowered the worker. All too often those who profess Jesus Christ (salvation) attempt to do His work without His sanctioning. The believer is to be prepared by/through the Holy Spirit to do the spiritual tasks on his agenda. When the disciples received the command of Jesus and obeyed the events of Acts 1:1-4, and the ensuing scriptures took place. "And when the day of Pentecost was fully come, they were all with one accord in one place. And suddenly there came a sound from heaven as of a rushing mighty wind, and it filled all the house where they were sitting. And there appeared unto them cloven tongues like as of fire, and it sat upon each of them. And they were all filled with the Holy Ghost, and began to speak with other tongues, as the Spirit gave them utterance." After the receipt of the Promise, the disciples were prepared to begin the works laid to their hands, which would be guided by the Holy Spirit. That day Peter preached Jesus Christ to the inhabitants and pilgrims in Jerusalem, and three thousand souls were added to the church (converted to Jesus Christ). At the receipt of Jesus Christ as personal Savior, the Holy Spirit and every other spiritual gift is added to the convert.

We teach, preach, minister, heal all by the power of the Holy Spirit. There are diverse gifts, of differing classifications; but they all come via one Spirit (1 Corinthians 12). The Holy Spirit manages the gifts dispensed by God, through belief in Jesus Christ our Lord.

Special Reference Notes

CHAPTER TWELVE:

What Christians Believe About...

LOVE

1. Name the "LOVE" chapter of the Bible._____

2. Fill in the blanks! "Whosoever _____ that Jesus is the _____ is born of God: and every one th at _____ him that _____ loveth him also that is of him." (1 John 5:1)

3. "By this we _____ that we _____ the children of _____, when we _____ _____ and keep his _____. (1John 5:2)

4. What did God, the Father do that showed his overt love for mankind? (Jn. 3:16)

   _____

   _____

   _____

   _____

   _____

   _____

5. "Beloved, if God so loved us, we ought also to love one another." Using the concordance, find this scripture.

   _____

   _____

6. In the "LOVE" chapter, what word is used to mean love?

   _____

   _____

7. Name the sixteen (16) attributes of love. (1Cor. 13:4-8)

(1)_____   (9)_____
(2)_____   (10)_____
(3)_____   (11)_____
(4)_____   (12)_____
(5)_____   (13)_____
(6)_____   (14)_____
(7)_____   (15)_____
(8)_____   (16)_____

8. Find and commit to memory 1 Cor. 13:13. Write it below.

_____
_____
_____
_____
_____

9. "_____ is love." (1 Jn. 4:8)

10. What are the four things Christians are supposed to do to their enemies?
    (Matt. 5:44)
    (1)_____
    (2)_____
    (3)_____
    (4)_____

11. Should we love everyone?   Yes   No   (circle one)

12. Is it okay not to love some? Yes   No   (circle one)

13. What must I do? (Lev. 19:18)

_____
_____
_____
_____
_____
_____

14. Which scripture ends, "...and pierced themselves through with many sorrows." (1Tim. 6:10)

_____

_____

_____

_____

_____

_____

_____

_____

_____

_____

_____

_____

15. Deuteronomy 6:4 says, "Hear, O Israel: The Lord our God is one Lord:"; verse 5 continues... "

_____

_____

_____

_____

_____

_____

_____

_____

_____

_____

_____

_____

_____

_____

_____

What To Do With Your Enemies

14 Bless them which persecute you: bless, and curse not.

15 Rejoice with them that do rejoice, and weep with them that weep.

16 Be of the same mind one toward another. Mind not high things, but condescend to men of low estate. Be not wise in your own conceits.

17 Recompense to no man evil for evil. Provide things honest in the sight of all men.

18 If it be possible, as much as lieth in you, live peaceably with all men.

19 Dearly beloved, avenge not yourselves, but rather give place unto wrath: or it is written, Vengeance is mine; I will repay, saith the Lord.

20 Therefore if thine enemy hunger, feed him; if he thirst, give him drink: for in so doing thou shalt heap coals of fire on his head.

21 Be not overcome of evil, but overcome evil with good. (Rom. 12:14-21)

With all of the problems that affect us, it is hard to keep the Christian principle of "love thy neighbor"; and even harder to "do good to them that hate you". We must figure out how to live here among mankind and still please the Lord. So I believe you need to know What To Do With Your Enemies.

Paul began this chapter with the admonition "I beseech you therefore, brethren, by the mercies of God, that ye present your bodies a living sacrifice, holy, acceptable unto God, which is your reasonable service. 2. And be not conformed to this world: but be ye transformed by the renewing of your mind, that ye may prove what is that good, and acceptable, and perfect, will of God." (Rom. 12:1-2)

He was of a mind to instruct those Christians at Rome in how to live as Christians and maintain the right relationship with God and man. The worldly always want the changed to return to their old ways and damning habits. Paul said do not conform to the ideas and works of the world, be different (transformed) by your thinking in an effort to please God.

The world has its own way of dealing with adversity and adversaries. The popular thought is to get even for everything. Now that we are saved and have new motives, we must learn what to do with our enemies. What To Do With Your Enemies?

We must bless them! The text begins, at verse 14. "Bless them which persecute you: bless, and curse not. 15. Rejoice with them that do rejoice, and weep with them that weep. 16. Be of the same mind one toward another. Mind not high things, but condescend to men of low estate. Be not wise in your own conceits. 17. Recompense to no man evil for evil. Provide things honest in the sight of all men."

Our hope is to be like Jesus Christ, for he is our ruler. He said, "By this shall all men know that you are my disciples, that ye love one another." You should know by now that you and the world are different. It hates you because you have changed back to your first love. 2 Cor. 5:17, "Therefore if any man be in Christ, he is a new creature: old things are passed away; behold, all things are become new." Since we are new creatures, we have new responses. When enemies attack, bless them.

Learn Not To Retaliate On The Same Level. (Rom. 12:18-19) "If it be possible, as much as lieth in you, live peaceably with all men. Dearly beloved, avenge not yourselves, but rather give place unto wrath: for it is written, Vengeance is mine; I will repay, saith the Lord." It is not always easy to overlook others' wrongdoing to you. Our natural response is to get even; at the very least, speak your mind on the subject. Paul said, "avenge not yourselves"; and that is very hard to do. You do not just let it go, "live peaceably with all men", and remember "Vengeance is mine; I will repay, saith the Lord." What To Do With Your Enemies?

Show Love to your Enemies! 'Therefore if thine enemy hunger, feed him; if he thirst, give him drink: for in so doing thou shalt heap coals of fire on his head. 21 Be not overcome of evil, but overcome evil with good." (Rom. 12:20-21)

When given the opportunity, show your enemies the Godly spirit that is in you. Treat them as you wish to be treated. If you want love, be loving. If Jesus is in you, then his spirit must be shown to others. "heap coals of fire on his head. Be not overcome of evil, but overcome evil with good." Mt. 25:45-46, "Verily I say unto you, Inasmuch as ye did it not to one of the least of these, ye did it not to me. And these shall go away into everlasting punishment: but the righteous into life eternal."

You may say, "How can I live like that, or how can I accomplish that". Well, Jesus Christ has already given us the perfect example. When he was in agony upon a Roman cross, he cried out "Father forgive them for thy know not what they do." He showed us how to forgive and have no malice for the enemy. Jesus had never sinned against anyone, but he wants to forgive everyone.

We must determine to love our enemies and to do good. "Bless them which persecute you: bless, and curse not." For the same Jesus who was crucified by mankind on trumped up charges was spat upon, lied about, scourged, beaten until his skin laid open and bleeding, mocked and scorned, betrayed, denied, and forsaken. Then he died for the sin of mankind, leaving an example for all man to follow. He was buried in a borrowed gave for three day and three nights. God dispatched an angel to roll back the stone from the grave; and Jesus rose from the dead with all power in heaven and earth. Power to live right, power to forgive, power to think right, power to save. Yes, Jesus still saves. "Come unto me all ye that labor and are heavy laden, and I will give you rest".

Special Reference Notes

CHAPTER THIRTEEN:
What Christians Believe About...
The CHURCH COVENANT

"The Church Covenant"

I.

Having been led as we believe, by the Spirit of God, to receive the Lord Jesus Christ as our Saviour, and on the profession of our faith, having been baptized in the name of the Father, and of the Son, and of the Holy Ghost, we do now in the presence of God, angels, and this assembly, most solemnly and joyfully enter into covenant with one another, as one body in Christ.

II.

We engage, therefore, by the aid of the Holy Spirit, to walk together in Christian love; to strive for the advancement of this church in knowledge, holiness and comfort; to promote its prosperity and spirituality; to sustain its worship, ordinances, discipline and doctrines; to contribute cheerfully and regularly to the support of the ministry, the expenses of the Church, the relief of the poor, and the spread of the Gospel through all nations.

III.

We also engage to maintain family and secret devotions; to religiously educate our children; to seek the salvation of our kindred and acquaintances; to walk circumspectly into the world; to be just in our dealings; faithful in our engagements, and exemplary in our deportment; to avoid all tattling, backbiting, and excessive anger; to abstain from the sale and use of intoxicating drinks as a beverage; and to be zealous in our efforts to advance the Kingdom of our Saviour.

IV.

We further engage to watch over one another in brotherly love; to remember each other in prayer; to aid each other in sickness and distress; to cultivate Christian sympathy in feeling and courtesy in speech; to be slow to take offense, but always ready for reconciliation, and mindful of the rules of our Saviour to secure it without delay.

V.

We moreover engage that when we remove from this place we will, as soon as possible, unite with some other church, where we can carry out the spirit of this covenant, and the principles of God's Word. Amen.

Basis of the Church Covenant

The obligations of Church membership outlined in the Covenant are all scriptural, as may be seen from the following study.

I. Salvation and Baptism.
   (Jn 1:11-12; Mt. 28:19-20).

II. Duties To The Church
   1. To walk together in Christian love (Jn. 13:34-35).
   2. To strive for the advancement of the Church, and promote its prosperity and spirituality (Phil. 1:27; 2 Tim. 2:15; 2 Cor. 7:1; 2 Pe. 3:11).
   3. To sustain its worship, ordinances, discipline and doctrines. (Heb.10:25; Mt. 28:19; 1 Cor. 11:23-26; Jude 3).
   4. To give it pre-eminence in my life (Mt. 6:33).
   5. To contribute cheerfully and regularly (1 Cor. 16:2; 2 Cor. 8:6-7).
   6. To carry my membership when I move, and be active in church work wherever I live (Acts 11:19-21; 18:24-28).

III. Duties In Personal Christian Living

1. To maintain family and secret devotions (1 Thess. 5:17-18; Acts 17:11).
2. To religiously educate the children (2 Tim. 3:15; Deut. 6:4-7).
3. To seek the salvation of the lost (Acts 1:8; Mt. 4:19; Ps. 126:5-6; Prov. 11:30).
4. To walk circumspectly in the world, and to be just in our dealings, faithful in our engagements and exemplary in out deportment (Eph.5:15; Phil. 2:14-15; 1 Pe. 2:11-12).
5. To avoid gossip and excessive anger (Eph. 4:31; 2 Pe. 2:21; Col. 3:8; Jas. 3:1-2).
6. To abstain from the sale and use of liquors (Eph. 5:18; Heb. 2:15).
7. To be zealous in our efforts for Christ (Tit. 2:14).

IV. Duties To Fellow Members

1. To watch over one another in love (1 Pe. 1:22).
2. To pray for one another (Jas. 5:16).
3. To aid in sickness and distress (Gal. 6:2; Jas. 2:14-17).
4. To cultivate sympathy and courtesy (1 Pe. 3:8).
5. To be slow to take offense, but always ready for reconciliation (Eph. 4:30-32).

Special Reference Notes

The Covenant: Keeping My Word

The Church Covenant is a voluntary agreement by members of a local church body who promise to conduct their lives in such a way as to glorify God, and promote the ongoing of His Church. Each member should study it carefully, refer to it often and seek to live by it daily. It clearly defines and outlines the obligations of church membership.

The Vow We Made "We do now in the presence of God, angels and this assembly, most solemnly and joyfully enter into covenant with one another, as one body in Christ. to walk together in Christian love;" This suggests a *vow*, a promise, an agreement with God and man. We should be careful to fulfill every promise made to the Lord and to our fellowman. Our word should be reliable. Vows (promises) are not made to be broken.

This portion of the Covenant deals with FELLOWSHIP and SERVICE. John 13:34-35, "A new commandment I give unto you, That ye love one another; as I have loved you, that ye also love one another. By this shall all men know that ye are my disciples, if ye have love one to another." We owe something to every person because of this scripture...LOVE. The disciples knew about the Ten Commandments, but Jesus said, "A new commandment I give unto you," which made them aware of the importance of love in the eyes of Jesus.

1 John 4:20, "If any man say, I love God, and hateth his brother, he is a liar; for he that loveth not his brother whom he hath seen, how can he love God whom he hath not seen?" It just does not make sense to hate mankind and talk about loving God. God is love and that same God made man.

Jesus commanded in John 15:9-10; 12, "As the father hath loved me, so have I loved you: continue ye in my love. If ye keep my commandments, ye shall abide in my love; even as I have kept my Father's commandments, and abide in his love. This is my commandment, That ye love one another, as I have loved you."

It's Not About Me "...to strive for the advancement of this church in knowledge, holiness and comfort; to promote its prosperity and spirituality; to sustain its worship, ordinances, discipline, and doctrines; to contribute cheerfully and regularly to the support of the ministry, the expenses of the church, the relief of the poor, and the spread of the gospel through all nations."

Phil. 1:27, "Only let your conversation be as it becometh the gospel of Christ: that whether I come and see you, or else be absent, I may hear of your affairs, that ye stand fast in one spirit, with one mind striving together for the faith of the gospel:" Ours is to live here together while focusing on God through Jesus Christ. We must take a back seat to the real meaning of Christianity...the study and work of Christ. 2 Timothy 2:15, "Study to shew thyself approved unto God, a workman that needeth not to be ashamed, rightly dividing the word of truth." 2 Cor. 7:1, "Having therefore these promises, dearly beloved, let us cleanse ourselves from all filthiness of the flesh and spirit, perfecting holiness in the fear of God."

All of the above leads us to revere the church, keep good relations with our fellowman, live in holiness, and put the church before our personal concerns. We must love the Church, and when we do; we will care for and give to the work and ministry of the Church. Giving is a blessed thing. It shows your commitment to God, and your willingness to believe, trust in and obey God. Remember, Jesus is the head of the church, and if we love him we must abide by his will.

Jesus died for the church that he came to establish in the hearts of man. He also left the church in the hands of man until he returns. Each of us will be held in account for our deeds, both good and bad. Jesus prepared the way for all believers and promised to come again. When he comes, I want him to say, "Well Done".

Special Reference Notes

CHAPTER FOURTEEN:
~ *The Answer Key* ~

Chapter One

1. Gen. 1:1, In the beginning God created the heaven and the earth.Ex. 3:13-14, And Moses said unto God, Behold, *when* I come unto the children of Israel, and shall say unto them, The God of your fathers hath sent me unto you; and they shall say to me, What *is* his name? what shall I say unto them? And God said unto Moses, I AM THAT I AM: and he said, Thus shalt thou say unto the children of Israel, I AM hath sent me unto you.

2. Gen. 18:14, Is any thing too hard for the LORD? At the time appointed I will return unto thee, according to the time of life, and Sarah shall have a son.Rev. 19:6, And I heard as it were the voice of a great multitude, and as the voice of many waters, and as the voice of mighty thunderings, saying, Alleluia: for the Lord God omnipotent reigneth.

3. Ps. 139:7-12, Whither shall I go from thy spirit? or whither shall I flee from thy presence? 8 If I ascend up into heaven, thou *art* there: if I make my bed in hell, behold, thou *art there.* 9 *If* I take the wings of the morning, *and* dwell in the uttermost parts of the sea; 10 Even there shall thy hand lead me, and thy right hand shall hold me. 11 If I say, Surely the darkness shall cover me; even the night shall be light about me. 12 Yea, the darkness hideth not from thee; but the night shineth as the day: the darkness and the light *are* both alike *to thee.*

4. Ps. 139:2-6, Thou knowest my downsitting and mine uprising, thou understandest my thoughts afar off. 3 Thou compassest my path and my lying down, and art acquainted *with* all my ways. 4 For *there is* not a word in my tongue, *but,* lo, O LORD, thou knowest it altogether. 5 Thou hast beset me behind and before, and laid thine hand upon me. 6 *Such* knowledge *is*

too wonderful for me; it is high, I cannot *attain* unto it. Isa. 40:13-14, 13 Who hath directed the Spirit of the LORD, or *being* his counselor hath taught him? 14 With whom took he counsel, and *who* instructed him, and taught him in the path of judgment, and taught him knowledge, and shewed to him the way of understanding?

5. Heb. 1:10-12, And, Thou, Lord, in the beginning hast laid the foundation of the earth; and the heavens are the works of thine hands: 11 They shall perish; but thou remainest; and they all shall wax old as doth a garment; 12 And as a vesture shalt thou fold them up, and they shall be changed: but thou art the same, and thy years shall not fail. Heb. 13:8, Jesus Christ, the same yesterday, and to day, and for ever.

6. 1 Kings 8:22-27, And Solomon stood before the altar of the LORD in the presence of all the congregation of Israel, and spread forth his hands toward heaven: 23 And he said, LORD God of Israel, *there is* no God like thee, in heaven above, or on earth beneath, who keepest covenant and mercy with thy servants that walk before thee with all their heart: 24 Who hast kept with thy servant David my father that thou promisedst him: thou spakest also with thy mouth, and hast fulfilled *it* with thine hand, as *it is* this day. 25 Therefore now, LORD God of Israel, keep with thy servant David my father that thou promisedst him, saying, There shall not fail thee a man in my sight to sit on the throne of Israel; so that thy children take heed to their way, that they walk before me as thou hast walked before me. 26 And now, O God of Israel, let thy word, I pray thee, be verified, which thou spakest unto thy servant David my father. 27 But will God indeed dwell on the earth? behold, the heaven and heaven of heavens cannot contain thee; how much less this house that I have builded? Jer. 23:24, Can any hide himself in secret places that I shall not see him? saith the LORD. Do not I fill heaven and earth? saith the LORD.

7. Deut. 33:27, The eternal God *is thy* refuge, and underneath *are* the everlasting arms: and he shall thrust out the enemy from before thee; and shall say, Destroy *them*. Ps. 90:2, Before the mountains were brought forth, or ever thou hadst formed the earth and the world, even from everlasting to everlasting, thou *art* God.

8. Lev. 19:2, Speak unto all the congregation of the children of Israel, and say unto them, Ye shall be holy: for I the LORD your God *am* holy. 1 Pe. 1:15, But as he which hath called you is holy, so be ye holy in all manner of conversation;

9. Mt. 28:19, Go ye therefore, and teach all nations, baptizing them in the name of the Father, and of the Son, and of the Holy Ghost: 2 Cor. 13:14, The grace of the Lord Jesus Christ, and the love of God, and the communion of the Holy Ghost, *be* with you all. Amen.

10. Jn. 4:24, 24 God *is* a Spirit: and they that worship him must worship *him* in spirit and in truth.

11. Gen. 1:1, 1:1 In the beginning God created the heaven and the earth.

12. Jn.. 3:16, 16 For God so loved the world, that he gave his only begotten Son, that whosoever believeth in him should not perish, but have everlasting life.

13. No! There must be a belief in the one who authored salvation, Jesus Christ (Jn, 3:16-17)

Chapter Two

1. the spiritual retrieval of man's soul from eternal destruction

2. Hebrews (Jews), the Children of Israel

3. to restore our relationship to God

4. God promised to send our deliverer, so He gave his own Son, Jesus Christ
   5. yes, Acts 4:10-12

6. Salvation came by way of the Son of God, Jesus Christ, the Messiah

7. no, only those who repent of their sins and believe in Jesus Christ

8. no, when one understands what Jesus has accomplished at Calvary and on Resurrection Day

9. Acts 4:12, "Neither is there salvation in any other: for there is none other name under heaven given among men , whereby we must be saved."

10. no: The Lord will never refuse anyone salvation

11. eternal life

12. Jesus became the sacrificial (Pascal) lamb, since blood atonement for sin was necessary. He orchestrated salvation for all who believe in his name.

13. It was that dreadful place where Jesus was crucified

14. no, no one can be saved by works, but by faith; it cannot be earned.

15. the Cross

16. no, see #22

17. spiritual rebirth

18. believing in and choosing Jesus Christ as Lord and Saviour, and allowing Him to alter the direction of your life

19. No! you must believe in Jesus Christ, the Redeemer

20. confession of self sin and belief in Jesus Christ as Saviour

21. no! the essentials for salvation are in #20, these mundane extras are man made and serve no spiritual purpose

22. no! a belief in Jesus Christ as Saviour is necessary, paramount.

23. nothing mankind can do is capable of saving souls; not worthy, because of sin

24. no, baptism alone cannot save; it is an act of obedience

25. no, we are not saved by works

26. absolutely, when he/she fulfills Christ's criteria

27. yes

28. yes, His own Son, Jesus, the Christ

29. no, because lower order animals do not have a soul to save.

Chapter Three

1. transgression of the law; all unrighteousness is sin

2. anyone who transgresses the law

3. EVERYONE

4. (a.) Satan (b.) Adam (c.) Eve

5. Adam was commanded by God not to eat from the tree in the middle of the Garden of Eden. He disobeyed, after being tempted by Satan, through his wife, Eve.

6. (a) sin (b) death (c) cursed (d) maternal travail (labor) (e) sorrow and labor (toil)

7. spiritual warfare within

8. yes

9. loss of paradise

10. human lusts

11. sin of omission

12. turn to Him, submit to Him and trust in Him for guidance

13. everyone

14. yea, only by the power which comes by the Spirit of God. We must submit to Him, and listen to His voice

15. certainly! we must ask forgiveness for sin and not repeat that sin, God forgives the penitent

16. sin causes death; spiritual death and all sin-debts get paid

17. yes, over and over

18. through Adam we are all sinful

19. we often elect to commit sin

20. omission, commission

21. yes

22. repent

23. Satan

Chapter Four

1. Seeking forgiveness for sins of omission and commission from God

2. Repent or perish; become sorry for sin

3. All who commit sin

4. The knowledge that we are sinful and that Judgment Day approaches; God's goodness leads to repentance

5. **A.** Yes! Luke 15:18

    B. When the prodigal cam to himself, Lk. 15:17

    C. He was humbled to a servant's mentality

    D. No, he saw himself as being loyal and earning his inheritance

    E. Yes, he should have repented of his malice and selfishness

6. **A.** Turn to God
    B. Repent and be baptized in the name of Jesus Christ
    C. Repent and be converted to blot out sin
    D. Repent and confess to be saved

7. Repent as often as necessary

8. Conversion

9. It is turning away from sin

10. Our appetites have changed. "Old things are passed away: behold, all things are become new". We become reconciled to God by Jesus Christ (v.18) God was in Christ, reconciling us to God and not charging our sins to us. Now we are ambassadors who work for God.

11. It is natural for flesh to sin, but all who love God must practice forgiveness; because it is God's way.

12. Yes! "For if ye forgive men their trespasses, your heavenly Father will also forgive you."

13. To save mankind from sin and sinning.

14. Repentance toward God and faith toward Jesus Christ

15. Except you repent, you shall all likewise perish

16. "As many as received him, to them gave he power to become the sons of God, even to them that believe on his name."

17. Believe and commit your life to God

18. Speak (confess) a and repent, turn to Jesus Christ

19. judgment day approaches, assurance has been given through Jesus Christ

20. seventy times seven; Matthew 18:21-22

Chapter Five

1. It is a declaration to the world that shows your death, burial and resurrection; and proclaims your vow to the Lord

2. Those who repent of sin and except Jesus Christ as Lord and Saviour

3. A. Father   B. Son   C. Holy Spirit

4. A. Death   B. Burial   C. Resurrection

5. A. Repent   B. Confess   C. Believe

6. The old man must die, be buried (submerged) in baptism; and be risen (resurrected) from the water to a new life.

7. No!

8. No, if it is possible, it must be done

9. No! We must hear and receive the Word of God, confess (repent) and be baptized.

10. We must believe on Jesus Christ, submit ourselves to water and be emerged or submerged into the water

11. No

12. God spoke, Jesus was in the water, and the Holy Spirit appeared in the form of a dove

13. Yes! They which is born of flesh is flesh, that born of the spirit is spirit

14. Father, Son and Holy Ghost.

15. One must be able to decide to accept Jesus Christ. He must also be able to repent.

Chapter Six

1. The New Testament commemoration of the Passover with Jesus Christ as the Pascal lamb; our blood sacrifice on the cross of Calvary

2. Jesus Christ instituted it at Passover with his disciples before his crucifixion

3. In Jerusalem, at Passover

4. A. Unleavened bread - the Body   B. Wine - the Blood

5. Bread, the marred body of Christ; the Wine, Blood shed for the remission of sin

6. No! They are merely symbols of the sacrifice made for the remission of sin- - by Jesus Christ

7. Yes! Read Acts 2:42; 20:7

8. As often as it is observed in the fellowship

9. A. No   B. No   C. No   D. No   E. No

10. Because Jesus has left it as a memorial

11. Matt. 26:18-29

12. A. Breaking of Bread

  B. Cup of Blessing

  C. eat the Lord's Supper

  D. the Lord's Table

13. Jesus commanded it

14. Not regarding Jesus' body

15. sample thoughts: forgiveness of sin, the crucifixion, Jrsus' sacrifice, God's love, etc.

Chapter Seven

1. your opinions

2. A. Sorrow over sin

  B. Seeking, asking of the Lord

  C. Showing appreciation (thanks)

  D. For others

3. C

4. Psalm 51

5. Yes, (see scriptures)

6. A. That the Father may be glorified in the Son

  B. That if two shall agree on earth

  C. If ye will abide in me, and my words abide in you

  D. If we ask any thing according to his will, he heareth us

7. Read them, make comparisons.

8. Yes

9. No

10. Praying was a daily Hebrew tradition

11. Jews prayed three times daily; 9 a.m., 3 p.m. and 6 p.m.

12. The Lord's Prayer

13. Our Father, which art in heaven...

14. 9, 9, 9, 10, 10, 11, 12, 12, 13, 13

15. Forgiving mankind will get forgiveness from God

16. Jesus' name

17. F A I T H

18. It is short and to the point; teaches forgiveness; teaches both moral and spiritual points

19. A. Ourselves

      B. One for another

      C. For the gospel

      D. For the sick

      E. For those in authority, for peace, and in thanks

      F. For your enemies

Chapter Eight

1. Hebrews

2. Eleven

3. "Now faith is the substance of things hoped for, the evidence of things not seen"

4. "Without faith it is impossible to please God"

5. your objective answer

6. Heb. 11:6 - "But without faith it is impossible to please him: for he that cometh to God must believe that he is, and that he is a rewarder of them that diligently seek him"

7. Paul

8. Yes

9. Works/ James 2:26

10. A. "For I say, through the Grace that was given unto me, to every man that is among you, not to think of himself more highly than he ought to think; but to think soberly, according as God hath dealt to every man the measure of faith"

    B. "Looking unto Jesus the author and finisher of our faith; who for the joy that was set before him endured the cross, despising the shame, and is set down at the right hand of the throne of God."

    C. "But the fruit of the Spirit is love, joy, peace, longsuffering, gentleness, goodness, faith, Meekness, temperance: against such there is no law.

11. Gospel; Jesus Christ; salvation

12. faith; faith; the just shall live by faith

13. "Therefore if any man be in Christ, he is a new creature: old things are passed away; behold, all things are become new."

14. Stephen

15. author and finisher of our faith

Chapter Nine

1. Stewardship is the ability to take care of, to care for,

2. The tithe of land is the Lord's (Holy); herds and cattle a tenth is holy unto the Lord, without redemption

3. Tithes, Offerings

4. The tenth portion belongs to God

5. Above the tenth portion are gifts of the increase

6. a. Burnt

   b. Drink

   c. Heave

   d. Meal

   e. Peace

   f. Sin

   g. Trespass

   h. Wave

7. The Work of the Church and the Ministry (Priests)

8. Robbery

9. Priests

10. Mal. 3:6, And I will come near to you to judgment; and I will be a swift witness against the sorcerers, and against the adulterers, and against false swearers, and against those that oppress the hireling in *his* wages, the widow, and the fatherless, and that turn aside the stranger *from his right*, and fear not me, saith the LORD of hosts.

11. Giver; 2 Cor. 9:7

12. Yes

    1. "Now concerning the collection for the saints, as I have given order to the churches of Galatia, even so do ye.

    2. Upon the first *day* of the week let every one of you lay by him in store, as *God* hath prospered him, that there be no gatherings when I come.

3. And when I come, whomsoever ye shall approve by *your* letters, them will I send to bring your liberality unto Jerusalem."

13. a. F

b. T

c. F

d. F

e. T

f. F

g. F

14. Yes,

15. The Lord's

16. (Information)

17. According to your blessings. Consider what God has done for you, and what he has provided for you.

18. A. 1 Tim. 5:17 Let the elders that rule well be counted worthy of double honour, especially they who labour in the word and doctrine.18 For the scripture saith, Thou shalt not muzzle the ox that treadeth out the corn. And, The labourer *is* worthy of his reward.

B. 9 Honour the LORD with thy substance, and with the first fruits of all thine increase: 10 So shall thy barns be filled with plenty, and thy presses shall burst out with new wine. 28:20 A faithful man shall abound with blessings: but he that maketh haste to be rich shall not be innocent..

Mal. 3: 10 Bring ye all the tithes into the storehouse, that there may be meat in mine house, and prove me now herewith, saith the LORD of hosts, if I will not open you the windows of heaven, and pour you out a blessing, that *there shall* not *be room* enough *to receive it.*

Luke 6: 38 Give, and it shall be given unto you; good measure, pressed down, and shaken together, and running over, shall men give into your bosom.

For with the same measure that ye mete withal it shall be measured to you again.

2 Cor. 9:6 But this *I say*, He which soweth sparingly shall reap also sparingly; and he which soweth bountifully shall reap also bountifully.

C. 2 Cor. 9:2, For I know the forwardness of your mind, for which I boast of you to them of Macedonia, that Achaia was ready a year ago; and your zeal hath provoked very many.

D. 2 Cor. 9:12 For the administration of this service not only supplieth the want of the saints, but is abundant also by many thanksgivings unto God;

E. Acts 11:29 Then the disciples, every man according to his ability, determined to send relief unto the brethren which dwelt in Judaea: 1 Jn. 3:17 But whoso hath this world's good, and seeth his brother have need, and shutteth up his bowels *of compassion* from him, how dwelleth the love of God in him?

19. A. 1 Cor. 16:2 Upon the first *day* of the week let every one of you lay by him in s tore, as *God* hath prospered him, that there be no gatherings when I come.

B. Mal. 3:8 Will a man rob God? Yet ye have robbed me. But ye say, Wherein have we robbed thee? In tithes and offerings.

C. 2 Cor. 8:7 Therefore, as ye abound in every *thing, in* faith, and utterance, and knowledge, and *in* all diligence, and *in* your love to us, *see* that ye abound in this grace also.

Chapter Ten

1. It is the confirmation of God's plan of salvation. It is the culmination to the prophecy about the Messiah.

2. Sadducees

3. Jn. 11:25, Jesus said unto her, I am the resurrection, and the life: he that believeth in me, though he were dead, yet shall he live:

4; No, Others had died, but salvation needed completeness and confirmation. It was prophesied that Jesus would rise from the dead.

5. Jn. 14:1-2, Let not your heart be troubled: ye believe in God, believe also in me. 2 In my Father's house are many mansions: if *it were* not *so*, I would have told you. I go to prepare a place for you.

6. Lazarus

7. here; Galilee

8. (1 Cor. 15:3-4) "1 Cor. 15:3-4, 3 For I delivered unto you first of all that which I also received, how that Christ died for our sins according to the scriptures; 4 And that he was buried, and that he rose again the third day according to the scriptures:

9. Resurrection, believeth

10. Lazarus, Bethany

11. Calvary, third

12. great, earthquake, angel, heaven, stone

13. Mt. 28:18, And Jesus came and spake unto them, saying, All power is given unto me in heaven and in earth.

Chapter Eleven

1. God, the Holy Spirit; the third person of the godhead (Trinity)

2. He is third person of the Trinity; the keeper, the comforter

3. A force; 16 And I will pray the Father, and he shall give you another Comforter, that he may abide with you for ever; 17 *Even* the Spirit of truth; whom the world cannot receive, because it seeth him not, neither knoweth him: but ye know him; for he dwelleth with you, and shall be in you.

4. 2 And the earth was without form, and void; and darkness *was* upon the face of the deep. And the Spirit of God moved upon the face of the waters.

5. Jn. 14:16 And I will pray the Father, and he shall give you another Comforter, that he may abide with you for ever;

6. Yes! Acts 2:1-4

7. He is to do what Jesus has left for Him to do.. Jn. 14, 15, 16

8. The Holy Spirit is in control of man. No, The Holy Spirit is here to do what Jesus Christ desires for our lives.

9. Yes.

10. Gal. 5:22-25, 2 But the fruit of the Spirit is love, joy, peace, longsuffering, gentleness, goodness, faith, 23 Meekness, temperance: against such there is no law. 24 And they that are Christ's have crucified the flesh with the affections and lusts.25 If we live in the Spirit, let us also walk in the Spirit.

11. 1 Jn 3:14, We know that we have passed from death unto life, because we love the brethren. He that loveth not *his* brother abideth in death.

12. No! When Jesus Christ is accepted as Lord and Saviour, all that he is comes upon the individual.

13. Yes

14. No

15. No; the Holy Spirit is not for our manipulation.

Chapter Twelve

1. 1 Corinthians 13

2. Believeth, Christ, loveth, begat, begotten

3. Know, love, God, love, God, commandments

4. For God so loved the world, that he gave his only begotten Son, that whosoever believeth in him should not perish, but have everlasting life.

5. 1 Jn. 4:11

6. Charity

7. (1) Suffers long

(2) Is kind

(3) Envies not

(4) Vaunteth not itself

(5) Thinks no evil

(6) Is not puffed up

(7) Rejoices not in iniquity

(8) Rejoices in the truth

(9) Bears all things

(10) Believes all things

(11) Hopes all things

(12) Endures all things

(13) never fails

(14) Does not behave unseemly

(15 Seeks not her own

(16) Is not easily provoked

8. And now abideth faith, hope, charity, these three; but the greatest of these *is* charity.

9. God

10. (1) Love your enemies

(2) bless them that curse you

(3) do good to them that hate you

(4) pray for them which despitefully use you, and persecute you;

11. Yes

12. No

13. 18 Thou shalt not avenge, nor bear any grudge against the children of thy people, but thou shalt love thy neighbour as thyself: I *am* the LORD.

14. 10 For the love of money is the root of all evil: which while some coveted after, they have erred from the faith, and pierced themselves through with many sorrows.

15. And thou shalt love the LORD thy God with all thine heart, and with all thy soul, and with all

Bibliography & Reference Sources

A New Baptist Church Manual
- Judson Press

Baptist Beliefs
- E.Y. Mullins

Baptist Church Manual (revised)
- J.M. Pendelton

Bible Study
- Harold L Willmington

Book of Bible LISTS
- H.L. Willmington
(Tyndale Publishers, Inc.)

Church Member's Handbook
- Joe T. Odle

Dake Annotated Bible (Commentary)
- Finis Dake

Survey of the Old Testament
- Paul N. Benware

What Baptists Believe
- Robert Smith, Jr.

The Daily Bible

The Holy Bible

S